To Chelsea

from

G. maw

# WASTED
# SPACE

# WASTED SPACE

## Judie Gulley

### illllustrated by
### Peter Catalanotto

Abingdon Press
Nashville

Wasted Space

*Copyright © 1988 by Judie Gulley*

Illustrated by Peter Catalanotto

All Rights Reserved

This book is printed on acid-free paper.

**Library of Congress Cataloging-in-Publication Data**

Gulley, Judie.
  Wasted space/Judie Gulley: illustrated by Peter Catalanotto.
    p. cm.
  Summary: Libby enters ninth grade with the awkwardness and
nervousness common to her age, determined to "fit in," stop befriending the
friendless, and be more socially successful.
  **ISBN 0-687-44060-2** (lib. bdg. : alk. paper)
  [1. High schools—Fiction. 2. Schools—Fiction.]
I. Catalanotto, Peter, ill. II. Title.
PZ7.G948Was 1988
[Fic]—dc19                                                      87-34174
                                                                    CIP
                                                                     AC

Manufactured in the United States of America

*For Ron and Jeff
super guys and good friends
who also happen to be
my sons*

# CHAPTER 1

Oh my stars, Persimmona!" Mom groaned, rolling her eyes back in the way I hate. She'd been rushing to get ready for work for the last half hour. Now she was on her knees trying to dig her red sandals out of the pile of shoes in the back hall, muttering, as usual, about my lack of cooperation with the housework. I'd been ignoring her, but the change in the tone of her muttering caught my attention. I stopped chewing my whole-wheat toast with red raspberry jam and looked up. She was staring through the bottom of the screen door.

"Why in the world can't you make friends with some *normal* people!" She whispered so loudly she might as well have shouted.

The hair on the back of my neck stood up and quivered. So did I. Through the screen, I could see my best friend, Kim Douglas, walking up the driveway, carrying her new books and notebooks. It was our first day of school—our very first day as high-school freshmen. She was wrapped in what had to be a flowered bedsheet, tied at the waist with a piece of clothesline rope. Gone was her silky dark hair that only yesterday had hung past her shoulders. A purple bandana—to match the flowers in the sheet, I suppose—was tied around her head and huge gold plates dangled from each ear.

Kim had been my best friend since last year when Mom and I moved into the old two-story farmhouse just down the country road from the Douglas house. I'd had all of eighth grade to get used to Kim's weird outfits. Even so, this one took my breath away. Still, I wouldn't let Mom know in a hundred years how I felt.

"What's wrong with Kim?" I said loudly. "At least she doesn't put on her eye shadow with a putty knife and smoke sixteen packs of cigarettes a day!" The best defense is a good offense, Kim always says.

Mom jumped to her feet, her cheeks reddening to clash madly with the russet eye shadow she'd caked on this morning.

"Anyway," I added as I grabbed my new notebooks off the table and prepared to flee, "if you wanted me to make friends with normal people, why didn't you give me a normal name?"

"Persimmona was my grandmother's name," Mom yelled, giving up all pretense of a whisper. "*She* was a kind, elegant, soft-spoken *lady*."

Meaning, of course, that I'm not any of those things. Still, I'd successfully drawn her attention away from Kim's outfit.

Kim tapped politely on the screen door. The gold plates thunked against her cheeks as she peered into the house. "Hi, Ms. Bradley," she said. "Libby ready?"

Mom's eyes narrowed. I'd never explained to her why Kim calls me Libby. It's because of what Kim says is my "Statue of Liberty" syndrome. SOL, she calls it. It's the something inside me that makes me want to gather in the "poor, the downtrodden, the huddled masses." Kim says all I need are sandals, a crown, and a lighted torch and I could decorate a harbor somewhere.

I bolted down the last of my toast and ran for the door before Mom could ask any more questions. A few feet down the gravel road, I finally managed to swallow.

"What are you doing?" I squeaked. "It's the first day of school, in case you've forgotten!"

Kim giggled. "Don't panic," she said, patting her head. "My hair is still under here—this is just a skull cap."

I breathed a sigh of relief.

"I've decided this semester I'm going to protest the religious harassment of the Persian Magi in Iran," she explained, with utmost sincerity. "Like it?"

Kim is always making a statement about some far out world problem. I started to roll my eyes, until I realized that's exactly what Mom would do, so I made a face instead. "Couldn't you have started high school a tiny bit less spectacularly?" I asked her. "What did your mom and dad say?"

Kim's dad is an executive with a farm equipment manufacturer and her mom is an RN with a high-powered cancer specialist in the city. Neither of them is into weird clothing.

Kim gave me a funny look and shrugged. "They're too busy fighting to notice what I wear," she said.

I could understand that. Mom and Dad had been divorced for three years, ever since I was eleven, but nothing will ever blot out the memory of those screaming, furniture-smashing years. They never seemed to realize I was around. Or care. Even now, just thinking about it makes me sick to my stomach, although my parents are pleasant enough to each other.

I guess it's easier for them if they only have to speak once a week, when Dad comes to pick me up on Saturday morning.

We came to the bus stop at the corner of our gravel road, where some kids were already waiting. I didn't actually see it, but I felt the crowd sort of lean away from us. I stood right next to Kim, my teeth clenched and my chin up. I was embarrassed for her and mad at myself for being embarrassed. She was my best friend. I wouldn't admit to anyone that sometimes she made me a little nervous, but there were times when I privately thought she could try to fit in just a little.

Over the summer, I'd made a resolution. This year I was going to make a sincere effort to fit in with the members of the freshman class. I knew I was just as good as the rest of them. There was no reason for me to be afraid to talk to anybody. Though of course, no one was the least bit interested in anything I had to say. And I was too tall. And my nose and feet were too big. And . . .

The bus roared to a stop in front of us, bright yellow and shiny. So optimistic, I thought. Clean windows even. We climbed aboard into absolute silence. Even Ms. James, the driver, had nothing to say. When I glanced back, she was staring at us in the overhead mirror.

I followed Kim to the middle section of the bus, where she hesitated. All summer we'd talked about how we were going to stroll right on through to the back seats, right past the middle seats where the junior-high "kids" sat. We were freshmen now—adults.

"Come on," Kim whispered. "There's a seat behind Rich Lawson."

I looked toward the rear of the bus at the eager,

snarling faces of the upperclassmen. My head started to pound. I could feel drops of sweat forming in my armpits. My feet were glued to the floor. So much for all my resolutions about fitting in. I shook my head. "I can't," I whispered back. Kim sighed. She plopped breezily down into a middle seat as though it were her *choice* and I slipped in beside her.

"All right, men, we're now taking bets."

I knew immediately who the voice belonged to—creepy Brian Lang.

"What are those strange creatures sitting with the little kids?" he went on. "Identify them and win the jackpot."

I was surprised to see the corners of Kim's mouth twitching. She turned around and looked at Brian.

"Stuff it, Donkeylips," she said sweetly.

Brian made gagging noises. I slid further down, hugging my notebooks to my chest. Kim looked at me and giggled. How could she think the whole thing was funny? I was so mortified I wanted to dissolve into the seat.

Brian's a junior, two years older than Kim and I, and absolutely the most gorgeous boy in the whole school. Also the biggest creep. Kim hates him—says he has no character. I think a guy who has Kim's kind of character has to wear braids and a dangly gold earring in at least one ear. None of the guys in our little country school is that liberated, so Kim doesn't date much. That's as much as I do, which is not at all, to be honest. She pretends not to care, but I kind of think deep down, she's as scared as I am.

Everyone else in our class is dating, some of them even going steady. I'm trying to accept the fact that I'm never in my whole life going to go out on a real date.

With a real guy, of course. A jerk like stupid Harold Crampton doesn't count.

Last year in eighth grade, when I decided I was in love with Harold, I didn't actually say to myself, "I'm in love with fat Harold Crampton." It's just the something that happens inside me. The SOL syndrome. One day, I looked at this lumpy, zit-covered dreg of humanity that no one else wanted and something warm stirred in my chest. Kim said it was muscle strain from all the bust-building exercises I do, and I should ignore it. Which of course I didn't.

As it turned out, my relationship with Harold was a great success and an even greater humiliation. In the beginning, I flirted madly with him, told him how wonderful he was—built up his self-confidence and all that. He was crazy about me. So crazy that he gave up his favorite things in the world for me—chocolate almond bars and hot fudge sundaes. His complexion cleared, he lost fifty pounds, bought a whole new wardrobe, and attracted the attention of Suzie Morland, who is a lifetime member of the "in" group—the ones who sit with Brian in the last four seats on the school bus.

It was just before eighth-grade graduation that Harold broke the news to me. "Persimmona, there's something I have to tell you," he began bravely.

I was pretty sure I knew what he was going to say. I'd noticed drool dripping down his chin every time he looked at Suzie. I tried tilting my head so that I was peeking through my eyelashes in what I hoped was a woman-about-to-be-wounded look.

"I'm taking Suzie to the graduation dance." It came out in a rush. He sighed and mopped his chin, obviously delighted that he'd done the *right thing*. Then he left. No "thank you for all you've done for me," "see you around," "you're a good person, Persimmona Bradley"—nothing!

Which is why I decided to rid myself forever of this Statue of Liberty sickness. Maybe I'm not really attracted to the losers I pick out. Kim says I just feel sorry for them. She says I have low self-esteem—that I feel I'm not as good as everyone else so I pick on the bodies no one else wants.

"Why else would you run around with me?" she says. In a way she's teasing. In a way, she's not. Sometimes, very privately, I wonder if she runs around with me for the same reason. Deep down, we're a lot alike, Kim and I.

I really can't explain what it is. Every time I see someone who doesn't fit in—kind of like me—I want to help that person somehow. It isn't something I plan, it just happens. In fifth grade Royal Martens was the original can't-walk-and-chew-gum klutz. Everyone made fun of him. I loved him. He *needed* me. I wasn't even embarrassed too much when I found the note in my desk that said, *"Persimmona loves Royal,"* with a hundred X's.

In sixth grade, it was Cash Walters. He came from a family of rodeo riders. His older brothers were named Rope and Tye.

Seventh grade was the pits. Mom and I moved, leaving behind all the neighborhood kids I'd grown up with. None of them had been good friends, but at least they'd known my name and there'd been a certain amount of comfort in that. After that, the whole year was a disaster.

Maybe that's why I fell so hard and fast for Harold. But good old Harold had *the end* written all over his formerly zit-covered forehead. Never again would I attach myself to some lonely being who desperately needed me. This year, even though it was getting off to a slow start, was going to be different. Right? Those kids in the back of the bus were just people. Just like me. There was no reason for me to be afraid to talk to them. Right?

I clutched my books closer to my chest and burrowed deeper into the seat, lost in the safety of my thoughts.

"Hey, look at the new kid. What a wimp!"

Brian's snicker brought me back to the real world. The bus brakes squealed. I saw a boy in the yard across the road hang a last item of wet laundry on a makeshift line that was strung from the old farmhouse to a huge oak. He scooped up a stack of books and ran for the bus, while Brian hooted some more.

"What a jerk," he said just low enough so the driver couldn't hear. "A laundry maid, no less!"

The boy walking to the bus was six feet tall at least. His white-blond hair badly needed cutting. It fell in heavy waves almost to his broad shoulders. Paint-spatter freckles covered his angular face.

The immaculate long-sleeve shirt he wore stopped two inches short of his boney wrists and huge hands. His faded jeans hugged his narrow hips but didn't quite come to the tops of his ragged tennis shoes.

As he stepped onto the bus, a wide grin split his cheeks into marvelous dimples. Even from where I sat, his palest-of-pale blue eyes sent goose bumps leap-frogging down my spine.

A pain began to spread through my chest from somewhere near my heart. Next to me, Kim sighed.

"Lib," she said. "I'll bet you've been doing those boob exercises again."

# CHAPTER      2

The new boy stopped on the top step and smiled at Ms. James.

"Mornin'," he said, in a velvet drawl that obviously didn't come from anywhere in Illinois. "Where should I sit?" Only it sounded something like, "Ware shoed ah see-it?"

It took me a minute to realize my mouth was open. I shut it quickly to keep from drooling.

"I sure hope he doesn't think he's going to 'see-it' back here," Brian said, just loud enough for the new kid to hear. The blond boy winced and his smile faded just a little.

In the overhead mirror, I saw Ms. James' eyebrows gather together over her nose in the expression we've all come to know and fear. Brian's smart remarks were bugging her. I knew she hated to send this new rider back to sit with him and the rest of the wolf pack, waiting eagerly to tear him apart. I heard muffled giggles behind me.

"Most of the highschoolers sit in the back," Ms. James said finally. "But you can sit up here for today, if you like."

The boy smiled his thanks and chose to make his way down the aisle toward the back. He tilted his head but his hair still scraped against the ceiling. The notebooks looked like postage stamps in his big hands. As he brushed by me, I wondered if he could hear my heart pounding. I rearranged my notebooks and cleared my throat to cover up the sound.

Before he could reach a back seat, his books were forcefully shoved from his grasp. They hit the middle of the aisle with a crash and slid under the nearby seats. I heard the sounds of feet kicking them even farther away. More giggles and nervous shuffling.

"Hey, creep, you dropped something." It was Brian. Kim grabbed the back of my blouse and hung on with a death grip. I wondered how she knew I was a heartbeat away from crawling under the seats to pick up the lost books. But the new boy's response puzzled me. Even though he was big enough to stuff Brian through a small side window with one hand, he didn't move. After a moment, he got down on one knee and gathered his books together.

"Sorry," he said quietly. "I'll try to be more careful."

"Better do that," Brian sneered. He always got really brave as soon as he found out whoever he was hassling wasn't going to punch him in the mouth. "We don't like slobs on this bus." He glanced around at the kids sitting near him, his chest puffing up a little. Some of the girls giggled loudly.

The howl of grinding gears brought everyone to attention. Judging by the way she sped around the corner, I could tell that Ms. James had heard everything. I knew she was smart enough not to interfere. If she stood up for the new kid, Brian and his gang would make it even worse for him. But her shoulders were set in a stiff, furious line and I had a feeling we were in for a wild ride.

The new kid climbed to his feet, walked back to a front seat, and sat down with two firstgraders. The broad shoulders looked perfectly ridiculous between the two little heads.

My heart did a complete flip-flop. I was lost. I knew it and so did Kim.

"Your torch is overheating," she whispered, finally letting go of my blouse. "Come on, Lib! Have you forgotten Horrible Harold so soon?"

I thought about that all the way to school. Funny how all my resolutions were going down the tube in one big sweep.

Ms. James slowed the bus as we drove into town and the high school came into sight. Our small school is a holdover from my great-grandmother's generation. Mom says the town officials make noises every year about tearing it down and putting up a one-story, modern building. And every year the older members of the community—who are also the most influential tax-payers—veto the idea.

I'm glad. I love the red brick building with its long, limestone-framed windows and elaborately carved entrance door. The only changes inside are the heavy glass doors on the remodeled principal's office, and private metal booths with doors inside the girls' john.

The rest of the inside is just as it was a hundred years ago. The twelve-foot ceilings, covered with patterned sheet metal, are painted white, and the wood floors are worn smooth from generations of kids shuffling between classes. The walls are always painted two-toned, in colors designed to make weaker stomachs go into convulsions.

I'd dreamed a lot about finally getting to h
and being a part of the beautiful one-hundred〜 ﹍-old
building. Now I was finally here. Big deal, right?

Ms. James steered the bus into the high-school
parking lot and braked to a stop—a little faster than
usual. She does that too, when she's mad. I stood up
too soon and wound up stumbling halfway down the
aisle to keep my balance. A huge hand gripped my arm
like a vise and steadied me.

"Careful," that rich velvet voice warned gently.

"Thanks," I gasped. I knew my face was probably
purple with embarrassment. My heart was beating so
fast I could barely breathe. I couldn't think of what to
say next, but I had to say something, so I blurted out
what I wanted to know.

"Who are you?"

The boy stood up and carefully inched past his little
seat partners. "I'm Randy Moe-gan," he said, walking
down the steps behind me. I turned at the bottom and
leaned one shoulder against the side of the bus—to
keep my knees from buckling, not to look cool. Kim got
off behind us, lifted her eyebrows at me, and strolled
into the front door of the school.

"Randy Mogan?" I repeated stupidly.

He grinned. "No—*Moe*-gan." Then he spelled it for
me. "M-o-r-g-a-n."

"Oh," I said, embarrassed again. I was at the end of
my conversation. There was a long silence, during
which I had to step away from the bus as it pulled
forward to leave the parking lot. Randy waited
patiently. Those sensational blue eyes looked at me and
right through me. After a moment, I realized my mouth
was open again.

"Uh, my name is . . ." I almost choked over it.

19

"Persimmona Bradley." He started to smile and I added desperately, "Everyone calls me Libby."

It wasn't true. Only Kim called me Libby. No one else even knew *why* she called me that.

"Pu-u-r-simmona." The word slid over his tongue as though he were tasting it. "I like it. Sounds like an old southern name," he said without a hint of ridicule.

"Is that where you're from?" I croaked. "The South?" Then mentally I beat myself over the head. Of course he was from the South. Stupid-stupid-stupid!

He nodded. "We're from Mizz-zippi," he drawled. "I lived in Guff-pote."

I got Mississippi all right, but I was darned if I'd ask him about Guffpote. My knuckles were beginning to turn white where I clutched my notebooks.

He looked at his watch. "Guess we'd better get inside," he said, much to my relief. "Can you show me where the office is?"

Oh, could I! The walk through the front doors and around the corner to the principal's office was short, but I tried to make the most of it. I pulled my shoulders back and swung my hips just a little. When he opened the door to the office, I suddenly couldn't bear to leave him.

"I'll wait here, if you'd like," I told him. "I'll be glad to show you where your first class is." I hoped desperately that I could remember where the rooms were. I'd only been in the building once before in my whole life, during registration last summer.

"I don't want you to be late," he said. His big smile was devastating. "Why don't you go on? I'll be all right." He said it, "Ah'll be awe-riot." He stepped into the office, then looked back over his shoulder.

"Thanks," he said. "I'm sure glad there's one friendly face on that bus."

Gelatin isn't the most original word to describe what my legs felt like as I walked to my first class, but it is the most accurate. Although I could feel a film of sweat across my forehead and my palms, my mouth was absolutely dry. I knew this was no Harold Crampton. Not by a long shot.

"Persim-*mon*-a" I whispered to myself, trying to catch the inflection that gave it such soft beauty when Randy said it. A boy standing at a hallway locker elbowed his friend and tipped his head in my direction. I ducked, and scurried around the corner out of sight.

"Dumb!" I breathed. "Why do you always do such dumb things?" Then I realized I'd done the dumbest thing of all.

I couldn't remember which way to go to my first class. The corridors on either side of me looked ominous and unfamiliar. From the drab army-green walls, portraits of past principals stared down at me accusingly. I wondered if there was some rule against school principals smiling for photos.

I hurried back and forth looking for the right room number until the halls were empty. My heart was pounding again, but this time it was with fear. I felt sick to my stomach. The bell rang and I was alone. For a long moment, I stood in front of an unfamiliar classroom door. I forced myself to turn the knob. The door swung open and bumped against the wall behind it.

The man sitting at the desk in the front of the room lifted his head to look at me, his eyebrows raised into question marks. Thirty faces turned toward me. There was absolute silence. I was frozen.

"Yes?" the teacher asked. "Can I help you?"

"I'm looking for freshman English?" I wondered if he could hear me.

The expression on the man's face bordered on exasperation. "Room one-ten, down the hall," he said, waving his arm vaguely. He dismissed me by turning away.

"Thank you," I choked. I fled to the door marked 110 and went through the whole procedure again. This time, I slipped inside and shut the door behind me.

"Are you in this class?" the large woman at the desk asked. "If you are, you're late."

I nodded. Guilty on both counts.

She looked over the top of her glasses at me. Her long hooked nose seemed to point back at her mustached upper lip and the flap of skin under her jaw jiggled every time she moved her head. I thought she looked like a vulture hovering over its prey.

Out of the corner of my eye, I saw a seat toward the back of the room. I edged toward it. The vulture frowned as she read her attendance sheet.

"Are you Persimmon Bradley?"

"Persimmona," I whispered. Someone in the back of the room snickered. Suddenly my name didn't sound so soft and pretty. Only dumb.

"Persimmona, try to be on time after this."

I nodded again and slid into the seat, trying not to make a sound.

What a great way to start the school year. The pencil I pulled out of my folder was dull, but no way was I going to walk up to the sharpener near the door.

I peeled the wood away from the pencil point with my fingernails, wishing the day was over so I could get back on the bus and stare at Randy.

If I'd known what was coming, I would have walked home.

# CHAPTER 3

I slammed my gym locker shut before the last bell quit ringing, and shot out of the locker room, silently thanking God that we didn't have to take showers on the first day of school. Tonight I'd worry about how to get out of exposing my body every day to the other girls in my gym class.

As we were changing out of our PE clothes, I'd risked a few glances at my classmates. It was as bad as last year—maybe even worse. I'll bet I was the only girl in the whole freshman class who was still trying to grow into a training bra. Even Kim wore a 32 AA.

Most of the girls were proud of their bodies and liked to parade around naked. How could every one of them have such perfect figures? Maybe I could send an anonymous letter to the teacher demanding curtains on the changing rooms and showers. It probably wouldn't make any difference. Besides, everybody would know right away who sent it. I was the only one in the whole gym class who used an industrial-sized beach towel in the shower room.

Ms. Martins, the gym teacher, said girls who were having their period would be excused from showering.

All we had to do was pencil in an M on the wall chart. The *wall* chart, would you believe! Up there for everyone in the world to see! My only other alternative was to break my ankle, which would be just as painful.

I hugged my books to my chest and scurried down the hall like a mouse being chased by a hungry cat. I never liked to wait around and take a chance that someone might actually try to talk to me. Not that anyone was likely to bother. Funny how easy my resolution seemed when I made it this summer. And how impossible it was now.

So what in the world was I going to say to Randy? Should I sit with him on the bus? Would he even want me to sit with him?

Often, I'd watched the popular girls sit with the boys and wondered what they found to talk about. They seemed to go on and on. I never could understand where they got all those words.

All I knew about Randy was that he'd moved from some funny-named town in Mississippi. Maybe I could ask him about his family. Did he have any sisters or brothers?

Mentally, I crossed off my own family life as a topic of conversation. Nothing to do handsprings about there.

Then I was hit by the most awful thought of all. What if for some reason he wasn't on the bus?

My heart started to pound so hard that I had to stop and lean against the wall next to the outside doors. People shouldered past me, heading for the long line of buses. But I couldn't move. I knew if I looked out and didn't see his beautiful blond head on old number nine, I'd die. I also knew if I looked out and *saw* him there, my knees would give out and I'd never make it to the bus at all.

"Hi."

It was him! The soft voice next to my shoulder startled me so badly that I dropped my books. Paper and folders and books scattered everywhere.

I looked up into Randy's face, and then down at the mess on the hall floor. It looked as if a tornado had struck. As he knelt to help me, I felt tears stinging my eyes. I could not—absolutely could not—do anything right.

"Hi," I managed to whisper and then "thank you," as he handed me a jumble of papers and books. Judging by the number of beads of sweat on my forehead, I decided my face had to be as gloriously red as the most impressive Illinois sunset ever.

Randy just smiled. I knew he was waiting for me to say something, but even though I stood there with my mouth hanging open, nothing came out. Finally he gave up, nodded at me, and pushed through the door. I watched him walk up the steps into the bus. He paused to talk to Ms. James.

"What happened to your stuff?"

I whirled and found Kim standing behind me.

"Oh Kim," I wailed. "What's the matter with me?"

"Nothing, I guess," she said, frowning. "You look just the same as you did this morning. What happened?"

"I just showed Randy Morgan what a stupid idiot I am," I sniffled as I tried to arrange the papers and folders and books in my arms.

Kim's frown turned into the smirky smile she uses when she tries not to laugh out loud.

"Who?" she asked. "Oh, that new kid? What did you do?"

I told her. She giggled. I wanted to kill her.

"Oh come on, Libby," she said, laughing. "Lighten up. I'll bet you dropped everything on purpose. What did you say to him?"

"My usual brilliant 'hi' and 'thank you.' And I didn't drop my junk on purpose, believe me. I wanted to die."

Kim's expression turned to complete exasperation. "Can't you see what a perfect chance you had? Guys love to play the big wheel and help a damsel in distress. Especially southern guys. You should have played it to the hilt."

She threw her head back, held her hand tipped out as though she had a long, elegant cigarette holder, and did an impressive imitation of a southern belle.

"Well, hell-low they-ah, Ran-dee," she drawled. "It certainly was sweet of y'all to help l'il ol' me. Oh mah stars, if you awn't jus' the handsomest little devil I evah did meet."

She was great. I started to laugh, but as I turned around, the sound froze in my throat, a sharp-edged cube of ice that I couldn't swallow. Randy was standing not five feet away, his hand still on the heavy glass door. This time his marvelous blue eyes weren't soft. They were cool and puzzled. Worst of all, I could see an expression that I recognized over all the others. I'd seen it in the mirror often enough. It was pain.

He nodded again and walked past us into the office. In a second, he came back out with a paper in his hand. This time he brushed by as though we weren't there.

I looked at Kim. She shrugged. I felt my fingers begin to prickle as if I'd touched a cactus plant.

"We hurt his feelings," I said.

Kim shrugged again. "I doubt it. Men aren't smart enough to get hurt feelings. Hey, come on! The buses are leaving."

She grabbed her bedsheet and ran for the bus, her sandals flapping madly on the sidewalk. I followed her, only my feet felt like lead and I barely made it before Ms. James pulled the door shut.

Maybe I could walk home, I thought wildly. It was only six miles. How could I face him? It wouldn't have been so bad, but he'd thought I was different from the rest of the kids on the bus.

And I'd meant to be.

In the end, it didn't matter. I pretended to be searching for something in my notebook as I shuffled past the front seat where Randy was sitting. After I crept into a seat with Kim, I decided that he hadn't bothered to look at me anyway, so it was all wasted effort.

A hundred different apologies tumbled one over another in my mind. But how could I ever get any of them out, even if I got a chance to talk to him? Silently, I mouthed the words again and again, practicing until I knew them by heart. There would be no mistake this time.

Kim looked at me and scrunched her nose up as if she thought I had something contagious.

"Lib, what the heck is your problem?"

"I've got to tell him I'm sorry," I whispered. "I'm going to change seats at the next stop and sit with him."

Ms. James yelled at anyone she caught switching seats. In the year she'd been my bus driver, she'd never once had to yell at me for anything. Sometimes I wondered if she even knew my name. But today, the first day of school, I was going to risk absolute mortification. I *had* to tell him I was sorry.

"If you're going to talk to him, you'd better shout," Kim said, nodding toward the front of the bus. I looked up just in time to see the back of Randy's head disappearing out the door.

He was getting off the bus at the first crossroad straight south of the high school. The Morgan place was a mile away, at the other end of the blacktop.

"But this isn't his stop!" I cried. I was frantic. I watched him walk away from us. His long hair swayed gently against his neck.

"That Statue of Liberty stuff is going to do you in," Kim whispered solemnly. "Mark my words."

Silently, I agreed. I was SOL all right, but not in the way she meant it.

Behind us, a window slid down with a bang.

"Hey, Creep!" It was Brian. "Got to get home early and scrub down the outhouse?"

Laughter and giggles echoed from the back seats. I recognized Harold's wheezy yodel. I wanted to wire his braces together.

Ms. James glanced up in her overhead mirror and gave us "The Look." Brian shut up, but I could still hear muffled giggles.

Randy didn't turn around. If he had, I might have been brave enough to wave.

# CHAPTER 4

Come on, Libby, cheer up." Kim poked me with her elbow. "By tomorrow, he'll forget all about it. Haven't I told you that there isn't a man alive who has an attention span any longer than an ancient hippopotamus's?"

She was trying to be nice and I managed a smile as I watched Randy's shoulders disappear down the blacktop road. By tomorrow, I'd have lost all my nerve to talk to him. The moment would be etched in stone and I wouldn't be able to take it back and make it right.

A blur of fenceposts and cornfields flew by the bus window. I saw myself reflected in the glass. Here I was, just a day into my resolution not to attach myself to some lost soul, and already I was mourning over this poor jerk. No, he wasn't a jerk. A person with those gorgeous blue eyes and that sweet way of talking could never be a jerk. Not even if he tried.

I moped all the way to our crossroad where Ms. James pulled the bus to a stop. There were seven of us who got off. We lived in both directions along the east-west blacktop that crossed the main road, all of us close enough to walk. The school district requested that we meet the bus at the corner to save Ms. James a lot of time.

Even though I complain long and loud with the others ("Everyone *else* gets picked up at the end of the driveway!"), I really do love the early morning walks.

On dark winter mornings, the only sound is snow crunching underfoot. The whole world is white and gray and black and brown. After a new snow, our country road is pockmarked with all sorts of little varmint tracks—rabbits, mice, raccoons, and various prints we can't identify. Sometimes we surprise a fat whitetail deer standing in the corn stubble. While we wait at the corner for the bus, we watch the sun come up in shades of red and lavender and gold.

Spring is fantastic too, rich with the smell of wet, plowed earth. The gravel road becomes an obstacle course of mud and puddles, but the bitter wind has turned into a gentle breeze. It doesn't claw at your face anymore, just dances around in your hair as though it wants to play.

I like all the seasons, but early fall is my favorite. The air is still warm, heavy and sweet with the pungent odor of woodstoves and burning leaves. There's a no-nonsense attitude about all the critters as they prepare for the winter ahead. The squirrels chatter at us as if offended when we disturb their work. I get a crick in my neck from watching flocks of Canada geese head south in their noisy, wavering V's high overhead.

Kim pretends to get tired of hearing me ooh and ah over everything, but I'm almost sure she shares a lot of my excitement. So much of Kim is hidden inside. She hasn't had the greatest life in the world, and she thinks that by keeping her feelings buried, they won't be hurt again.

Sometimes I think she's right. Mom says I wear my heart too close to my skin. I guess it's true, because I sure get my feelings hurt a lot. But maybe Kim does too. Maybe she's just better at hiding it.

One October morning we saw a mother fox and two half-grown kits playing in the leaves. They jumped and rolled and chased one another as though they were all babies. Kim and I sat in the weeds by the side of the road and watched. Once Kim looked at me. Her eyes were wide and round and under all the silver eye shadow, I could see into her soul. "Aren't they wonderful?" she whispered.

I nodded solemnly and we just sat there grinning stupidly at each other.

"I wonder why the mother fox plays with her babies like that," I whispered after awhile.

Kim shrugged as she always did. "Maybe because they're almost grown up and she knows it won't be too long before they leave her."

I thought about that for a long time. Kim is pretty good at figuring things out.

She hadn't convinced me about the ancient hippo bit, though. Today, as we trudged up the road toward home, I had a feeling Randy would remember our little offense for a long time. I knew I would.

I worried out loud and Kim shook her head in exasperation. Bad as I felt, I still laughed when the huge earrings swung around and smacked her in the face.

"Good grief!" she muttered, rubbing her nose. "I was hoping you were finally over all this nonsense. Harold the Hun didn't teach you a thing."

"I just can't stand hurting someone's feelings," I said. "I know how it feels."

"Hey, do you think for a second there's a man on

earth who would feel a gram of guilt after tearing *your* feelings to shreds?" she demanded. "Men just aren't made the same as females."

"I know that," I said with a small grin, glancing sideways at her.

"You know what I mean," she said crisply. She hated it when I managed to dent her cool in the least. "We didn't do any permanent damage to ol' Mizz-zzippi's delicate little psyche. Believe it."

We'd reached the top of the small hill away from the corner and I could see a car in the driveway of our faded-white farmhouse.

"That your dad?" Kim asked.

"Yeh," I answered, already uneasy.

I couldn't remember his ever stopping by on a weekday. I gripped my books tightly and jogged up the shoulder of the road. Kim waved good-bye at the mailbox. I was almost to the shiny maroon sedan before I saw the head in the passenger side of the front seat. It definitely wasn't Dad's.

"Hello," the woman said. She was blonde and dark-eyed and very pretty. Expensive-looking earrings sparkled on her earlobes. Her makeup was just right. "Your father's in the house," she said, with a big smile. I passed her without saying anything and slammed the screen door hard behind me.

"Hi, P J," Dad said from the dining room. He moved quickly away from the old desk in the corner, as though he'd been looking at something he shouldn't have. "How're you?"

"Hi, Daddy," I said, putting my books down on the dining room table. "I'm fine."

I felt the same thrill that I feel every time I look at him. He's the most beautiful man I've ever seen. His eyes are a deep rich brown, like chocolate fudge, instead of washed out and muddy like mine. His thick, wavy hair is salted with just the right amount of gray. It makes him look wise and mature. He works hard at keeping his stomach flat and worries constantly about what he weighs.

I've always wished I could run to him and hug him with all my strength but he thinks hugging is something you do to babies. He made a kissing noise at my cheek and moved away, examining with great interest the cheap imitation oil painting Mom had hung behind the sofa.

"Mom won't be home until five," I told him, twisting my fingers behind my back until they hurt.

"That's all right," he said, still ill at ease. "I really came to see you. How was school today?" He sat down on the arm of the sofa. He was trying to make small talk, something he never does with me. A warning bell went off inside my head. Suddenly the room seemed very small and close.

"O.K." I looked down at my shoes and studied the toes.

"Probably got a boyfriend this year, huh? A young lady as pretty as you?"

I felt my cheeks redden. I shrugged, wishing he'd get to whatever it was he'd come to tell me.

"Well . . ." he cleared his throat and stared up at the ceiling. This was the very same problem we have when he picks me up on Saturday. After, "Hi, how are you?" and "I'm fine," we have nothing to say to each other. Usually he takes me to a show so we don't have to talk. I wish I could make our visits more fun for him but I don't know what to do or say. I always have the feeling that it's a great relief to him each time he drops me off on a Saturday night.

After he drives away, I always run upstairs and lie across my bed so that I can look out the window and watch his red taillights go down the highway. Each time, I vow I'm going to be exciting and talkative the next weekend when he picks me up. A week later, I spend all Friday night trying on outfits and setting my hair. Saturday morning, I'm awake at dawn and dressed hours before he drives in the driveway.

And each time, I get in the car, he says, "Hi, how are you?" and I say, "Fine."

Today I had a feeling there was something important about to happen. Why else would he be here? His eyes shifted as he glanced at me and then away trying not to get caught.

"Well . . ." he said again.

"That's a deep subject," I said, and tried a smile. He looked at me blankly. I felt a stone settle into my stomach.

"P J, I guess I ought to come right to the point." His voice became brisk, almost businesslike. "I've been offered a terrific promotion by my firm . . . an office and secretary of my own . . . a lot more money."

"That's great, Daddy!" I really meant it. I could see the excitement in his eyes.

"Honey, it's in Florida."

For a moment, I couldn't understand what he was telling me.

"Florida?" I said stupidly. "How will I see you on Saturdays?" Then it sank in.

"Oh," I said. I tried hard to keep my face smooth. "Well" (a deep subject, I thought wildly). Then I managed to ask almost calmly, "When will I see you?"

He shrugged, a trapped look coming to his eyes. "I don't know, Sweetheart. I'll be pretty tied up for

34

awhile. Sharon and I will have to find a house." He hesitated. A pink flush spread up his neck. "Uh, Sharon's going with me. Did you meet her? She's out in the car."

I didn't answer him. "When are you going?" I asked instead.

He stared at the ceiling and took another deep breath. "Well, we'll probably leave tonight or early in the morning."

"Oh." I couldn't think of another word to say.

"But I'll be back as soon as I can," he rushed on. "And I'll write every week. And maybe you can come down over Christmas vacation. Wouldn't that be fun? . . . spending Christmas in Florida?"

I nodded. He stood up and I could see the same relief in his eyes that I saw every Saturday night as I got out of the car. Funny. He looked just like Harold Crampton after Harold had told me he was going to the dance with Suzie.

"So, all right. You be a good girl, O.K.? Get good grades and mind your mom." He squeezed my arm. "I'll see you again as soon as I can."

I stood behind the screen door and watched as he backed out of the driveway. The woman waved but I didn't wave back. I wondered what was so different about her that made him like her and not Mom.

If it'd been night, I might have cried. But somehow, it didn't seem right crying on a bright, golden September afternoon. I went outside and sat on the step, crossing my arms tightly about my chest—trying to hold all of me inside.

# CHAPTER 5

I was still on the step when Mom's old rattletrap roared into the driveway, dust foaming up from under the bald tires. The muffler—what was left of it—was hanging loose underneath, clattering loudly against the gravel.

She laughingly calls her car Frog, and believe me, the name fits perfectly. It's a lumbering green four-door, covered with rust spots. The springs are so bad it squats low to the ground. I'm embarrassed to be seen in it, but Mom is more practical. She says it doesn't matter what it looks like. All she wants is a car that starts and takes her where she wants to go. It does that, I guess. Most of the time.

Sometimes though, I see a funny look in her eyes when she looks at Dad's gleaming maroon sedan, but she doesn't ever say anything. Actually, she says very little about Dad. I guess it's because of one of her favorite sayings: "If you can't say anything nice . . ."

She stopped the car next to the corner of the house, got out, and pulled a sack of groceries from the back seat. As she walked toward me, I tried to figure out what it was about her that had made Daddy stop loving her.

I guess it was the only way to keep from thinking about why he'd stopped loving me.

It couldn't be because she's not pretty, because she's beautiful, one of the most beautiful women I've ever seen, although I wouldn't ever admit it to her. Just lately, she's had her honey-blonde hair cut in a short, blunt style with bangs that sweep across her forehead. She says she's trying for a "look." I like it. It frames her face into a heart shape and emphasizes her huge brown eyes. Her skin is perfect—under all that makeup, that is. I accuse her of putting eye shadow on with a putty knife. I know that's one way to really get her goat. She gets absolutely furious, and for a few days, the eye shadow is spread on thicker than ever—to irritate me, I'm sure. You'd think after awhile I'd wise up and keep my mouth shut, but I've never been known as a fast learner.

Maybe she's a little heavy through the hips, but her waist is smaller than mine, and all in all, her body is great. She knows how to dress like a million dollars, even though most of her clothes are bought on sale at the local discount store.

I can't understand why I didn't inherit just a little of her figure. I haven't been able to fit into her size 9 clothes since I was in fifth grade. She wears a size 5 shoe, which is another irritation to me when I compare her dainty feet to my built-in snowshoes. And I have no hope at all of ever being able to trade bras with her. It just isn't fair.

Which brings up another of her favorite sayings. "Persimmona," she says. "No one ever promised that life would be fair."

Six months ago, she was a happy person, laughing and singing for no reason at all. That was before she started working mornings as a cashier at Eagles grocery store, afternoons for the *Johnston Daily News*, and going to journalism classes at night. Now it seems as if she's tired all the time.

She's always wanted to be a writer and when the *Daily News* first asked her to do some articles, she jumped at the chance. They turned out pretty good and she enjoyed them so much, she decided that newspaper work would be her career. The weekly check from Eagles pays our rent and buys groceries, but she's hoping that soon she can make a living with her writing.

I do too. Maybe when she quits one of her jobs, things will be different between us.

Now she's hardly ever home. When she is, she's so grouchy that we can't even speak to each other civilly. I admit I don't try too hard. At least, I've given up saying anything about how short-tempered she is, even though she says the fights are as much my fault as they are hers.

"Can't you be a little more understanding, Persimmona?" she says.

When I complain that she's never home, she doesn't argue. She just begs me to be patient.

"I only need two years of journalism to be eligible for an editor's job," she says. "Can we both just hang on for two years?"

What else can I do? Sometimes, though, I feel as if I'm losing my handhold.

Mom stopped at the backstep where I was sitting and shifted the bag of groceries to her other arm. She looked down at me curiously. Ever since I was little, she's been able to tell when something has been wrong in my world. It's a fault I try hard to correct.

I tried to swallow the lump in my throat. Really, I love her. Why do we always have to fight? She was trying so hard to make something of her life and raise a daughter at the same time. Was I a disappointment to her?

"Hi, Sweetheart," she said. Her voice sounded exhausted. "Open the door for me, will you?"

I did and as she brushed by me, I could smell her perfume, the stuff I hated. I wrinkled my nose and she frowned.

"Oh come on," she grouched. "Let's not start that again."

"What?" I asked, louder than I'd intended. "Start what?"

"You know! Smart remarks about this perfume. Just because Carl bought it for me . . ."

"It's not because he bought it," I argued, even though I knew it was. "It reeks!"

Creepy Carl was the latest on Mom's short list of boy-friends. He wasn't the worst one, but close. He was tall enough to play major league basketball, and had a large stomach that sort of extended from his chest and overlapped at his belt, which he wore up under his armpits. But the worst thing about him was his hair. He wore it below his ears in a style that was out of style five years before. And he let one side of it grow twice as long as the other, then combed it straight across his head to cover the bald spot on top. He smiled a lot and patted the top of his head every few minutes to make sure his scalp wasn't showing.

"Can't you at least go with a guy that has a little class?" I muttered. I was mad at myself for saying it. If Kim had been there, she'd have told me I was striking out at the wrong person—that it was really my father I was angry with. Sometimes I think she's practicing to be a psychiatrist.

"My stars, Persimmona!" Mom said, pulling things out of the sack and slamming them down on the table. "You'd think I could walk in the door after working my tail off all day and be greeted like a human being."

"Maybe if you'd act like a human being!" I shouted. "No wonder Dad's moving to Florida . . ."

I turned away, biting the edge of my lip so hard I could taste blood. Why had I said it like that? Whywhywhy!

"What! What did you say?"

Mom grabbed my arm and pulled me around. Her face was white, tinged with crimson spots on her cheeks. Her warm brown eyes had turned icy and black looking. "Robert's moving to Florida?" It came out like a hiss.

I nodded.

She let me go. Her small hands balled into fists and she slammed them down on the table.

"Damn him!" she whispered. "When?"

"He was here this afternoon," I told her. "I think they were planning to leave tonight."

"They? *They?*"

Somehow I managed to nod again. "Her name is Sharon."

"I *know* what her name is!" Mom kicked the kitchen chair. It slid across the cracked linoleum and banged into the basement door. "That spineless no-good excuse for a man!" she raged. "That'll be the end of the child support! And he owes me five months' right now."

She continued to shout as though I weren't even there. After awhile, I opened the back door.

40

"I'm going for a bike ride," I said, and slipped outside. I knew I'd whispered and I didn't know if she heard. It didn't matter. I didn't matter. Only the money.

I climbed on my old green three-speed and steered it down the driveway onto the gravel road, not even trying to miss the big rocks. Who cared if one of the tires went flat! Who cared, who cared.

No one no one no one, the swish-swish of the bike tires talked back to me. The wind pulled the tears out of my eyes and back into my hair. I pedaled faster and faster, gritting my teeth as I slid around the corner onto the blacktop and shifted into third gear. The cranks groaned and creaked as I put my head down and pushed even harder.

I pretended I was on a trip. Somewhere at the end was a place where a band was playing to announce my arrival. Flags flying. People cheering. A destination. All I had to do was to get there and I'd live happily ever after. My feet were flying. I was gasping for breath. I welcomed the pain in my chest.

I didn't even see the red truck.

The howling screech of locked brakes was my first clue I was in trouble. I jerked my head up to see a red blur sliding toward me. Without thinking, I wrenched the handlebars to one side. I felt the tires sloughing in the dirt on the shoulder on the road and then the bike disappeared out from under me. For an eternity, I tumbled through a silent sky, lights and colors awash about me. The bone-jarring thud when I hit the ground brought me back to reality. For another second, I slid and rolled through the gravel along the shoulder. Finally, everything stopped. My face was buried in the wet weeds. I kept my eyes tightly shut, wondering if I was still alive.

But I could hear the crickets chirping again. Across the road in the tall corn, a meadowlark warbled happily as though nothing had happened. When a door slammed, I tried to move. Running footsteps crunched in the gravel on the side of the road. Gentle hands touched my back.

"Are you O.K.?" The anxious voice made me want to shrivel up to nothing and disappear. "Persimmona, are you O.K.?"

Raw spots on my elbows were beginning to burn. There was something warm and sticky running from my knee down my shin to my ankle. I rolled over and opened my eyes. The voice, oh dear God of course, belonged to Randy Morgan.

# CHAPTER _____ 6

I closed my eyes again. "Please God," I prayed silently. "Let this just be a minor nightmare." But I was pretty sure that when I opened my eyes, Randy would still be there. He was.

"Are you all right?" He repeated.

"Sure," I said, pushing myself into a sitting position. "When you barrel through life as I do, you have to get used to sudden stops." I brushed at the dirt and grass on my blouse, not daring to look up to see if he smiled.

I couldn't believe it! The most embarrassing moment of my entire life and *he* had to be the one who saw the whole thing!

Both of my elbows felt like raw meat, and there was a hole in one of the knees of my good jeans. Through the hole, my kneecap looked like hash. This guy had to think I was the biggest jerk ever. Still, the physical pain was a relief compared to the knife that had been twisting in my heart. I couldn't believe how much better I was beginning to feel. I wondered if it was because Randy was breathing on my neck as he examined my elbows.

"You rode right out in front of me," he said, picking a

weed out of my hair. "Scared the pants right off me."

Bad choice of words for my complexion, but he didn't seem to notice.

"Sorry about that," I said, and before I could stop myself I was blubbering on. "I'm sorry about today, too. You didn't hear what you thought you heard."

A smile touched the corner of his marvelous mouth. "All right, what did I hear then?"

I stared at him helplessly. How could I tell him I thought he was the most wonderful thing in the world? That I loved him? That I wanted to marry him and have twenty kids? And . . .

I knew if Kim had been there, she would have stuffed my torch in my mouth.

"Kim was just being silly," I said finally. "We didn't mean for you to hear."

Randy smiled full out. My heart kicked itself off my rib cage and vibrated like a harp string.

"'Sokay," he said. "Can you stand up? I'll take you back to my house and we'll clean you up a little."

I opened my mouth to protest. I couldn't let his whole family see how dumb I'd been, but when he pulled my bike out of the ditch, I knew I didn't have a choice. The front tire looked like a piece of overcooked spaghetti.

"I think the rim's O.K.," he said after a brief examination. "I can relace the spokes in no time at all." It sounded something like "no tom tall." I had to listen hard to pick up every word. He took my hand and helped me to my feet. My fingers were on fire with more than gravel burn.

I climbed into the battered old red pickup. He started it, shifted into gear, and turned it around in the middle of the road, heading back toward his house.

I stared out the windshield, trying desperately to find

45

something—anything—to say to him. Finally I blurted out, "You got off the bus early today." I instantly regretted it. "I'm sorry," I said quickly. "I don't mean to be nosy."

"I can get home forty-five minutes earlier that way," he said with a shrug. "No sense riding all the way around just to be dropped off in my driveway."

"Do you like walking?" I was really hopeful. Maybe we had one thing in common.

"Sure. Besides, Dad needs me to help out at home." He glanced at me. "My mom is sick."

"Oh, that's too bad," I said. "I'm sorry."

He turned into his driveway and I was saved from having to think up something else stupid to say.

A tall, thin man was bent over the engine of an old car in the driveway. As we braked to a stop he stood up, wiping his hands on his greasy coveralls. His smile was big and warm and I saw Randy in every move he made.

"Looks as if I need to have a talk with you, boy," he said. "I send you to the store for an oil filter and what do you bring back? . . . a gorgeous young lady."

Why am I blessed with this marvelous blushing reflex that turns my face purple every time someone says something nice to me?

"Th-thank you," I stammered, not sure if I should thank him or not. He looked at me expectantly, his eyes taking in the grass stains and blood on my clothes. I would have told him my name but it had slipped my mind for the moment.

"This's Persimmona Bradley, Dad." Randy came to my rescue. "I met her on the bus this morning. She lives just down the road a piece. She had a little trouble with her bike on the blacktop."

I managed to nod and say, "It's nice to meet you, Mr. Morgan." At least, I think I said it out loud.

Randy took my arm and tugged me toward the house. "I'll show you where you can wash up some," he said, "while I work on your rim."

He led me through the back door of the brown-sided, two-story farmhouse. I knew this house had once been part of a small farm, just as ours had. When the big farmers gathered the little family acreages in, they often rented the old houses out, rather than let them go to ruin. The houses were huge overall, but cut up inside into many little rooms, like ours. Someone had done some remodeling on the Morgan house. The kitchen was fairly new and modern, with bright, flower-patterned wallpaper.

I was surprised by the dirty dishes stacked in the sink and food that was obviously left over from breakfast still sitting on the table. The stove was spattered with grease. I could tell someone had made an effort to clean it, but had only succeeded in smearing the grease around. If I hadn't known better, I'd have thought the two men lived here alone. Randy had said his mother was sick, but this looked like a long-term mess.

Randy wasn't the least bit embarrassed. He showed me to the bathroom, just off the kitchen, and it was in pretty much the same dismal mess.

"I'll be in the garage," he whispered, holding a finger to his lips. "Mom's asleep."

I nodded. When he left, I locked myself in securely and dabbed at the scrape marks until I removed most of the gravel and dirt. My elbows were just scratched on the surface, but my right knee was hurt worse than I'd thought. I winced as I tried to soak the dried blood from the shredded flesh. It really hurt, but I was cheered by

47

the thought that it was good for at least two week's excuse from showering in gym.

When I was done, I opened the door and tip-toed across the kitchen. As I reached for the back door, I heard a rustling noise from the next room.

"Hello?" a voice murmured. "Is someone out there?"

I froze with my hand on the doorknob. What should I do? Would Randy and his father be angry with me because I'd caused Ms. Morgan to wake up? I cleared my throat.

"It's just me," I called.

A soft chuckle came from the darkened room. "Well, 'Just Me,'" the voice said, "come in here for a second."

I stood in the doorway and waited until my eyes adjusted to the dim light. Lying in the huge bed across the room was the most beautiful woman I'd ever seen. Her hair wasn't quite as white-blonde as Randy's, but it hung in the same soft waves clear to her shoulder blades. Her eyes were even a paler blue than her son's, and they were framed by long golden lashes. Her skin was white—almost transparent—and flawless, without a hint of makeup. She switched on a lamp next to the bed, and when she smiled at me, I could see her teeth were small and even and perfect.

"Come here, Sugar," she said, holding out a slim white hand. It came out as "Come heah, Shu-gah."

"My," she said, looking me up and down when I stood next to the bed. "Don't you know but you're a pretty one."

This absolutely fantastic person was telling me I was "pretty"? I was stunned. I couldn't even say thank you. She didn't seem to notice. She took my hand and hers was unbelievably smooth and warm.

"Are you a friend of Randy's?" she asked, her marvelous eyes searching my face.

"Y-yes," I squeaked. "I live on the next road. I mean . . . ah . . . my name is Persimmona Bradley."

Her smile broadened and her eyes twinkled with turquoise lights. "I knew a girl as fetching as you would have a lovely name," she said. "Persimmona." She tasted it on her soft lips. "Persimmona, sit down and talk to me for a second." Her voice had a lovely southern melody, yet the words were clear and easy to understand.

I was transfixed. When she patted the chair next to the bed, I sank into it without a murmur.

"Now tell me," she continued in the same honey-rich drawl. "Tell me where you live and about your mama and daddy."

I was like a little marionette. I told her everything about my family, right up to and including the part about my dad leaving for Florida today and how I felt about it. My mouth ran as though it were motorized and the off switch were broken. Her face was so open and her eyes so sympathetic that I couldn't stop the tears when I finally managed to clamp my jaws together.

"Oh, I'm sorry," I cried. "I'm so stupid. I didn't mean to . . ."

She was still holding my hand, and she squeezed gently. "When a body's had her feelings hurt, sometimes it helps to tell someone," she said. "Don't you think?"

I nodded. I adored her.

She looked over my shoulder and smiled. "Hello, Sweetheart," she said. The love in her voice flowed and swirled gently about me like a warm, softly scented river.

Randy walked in and stood by my elbow. "'Lo, Mama," he said. He bent to kiss her cheek and touched her hair.

"Did you have a good day in school?" she asked him as he smoothed the blankets about her.

"Sure did," he answered, glancing quickly at me. "No problem. Guess I'll get along real nice."

She released my fingers and sank back on the pillows with a sigh. Her eyes closed and the long lashes fluttered on her cheeks. "I feel guilty, you know," she said. "Making you change schools again."

"Don't think about it another second, Mama," Randy said. "I like it much better here. Small school and all. I can get to know everyone this way."

Ms. Morgan smiled softly. "You've already made one nice friend," she said. "I like you, Persimmona Bradley. I surely hope you'll come visit again."

Randy touched my shoulder and tipped his head toward the door. I stood up.

"I will, Ms. Morgan," I told her eagerly. "I'll be glad to." I meant it.

I followed Randy out to the garage. The bike tire looked like new.

"I'll give you a ride home," he said. "It's getting too dark for you to be out on the blacktop."

I would have protested, but my knee had stiffened so badly I wasn't sure I could even pedal. He didn't give me a chance to refuse, anyway. He just lifted the bike into the back of the truck.

"Your mom is sure nice," I said, as we drove out of his driveway. "And beautiful, too."

He glanced at me and smiled. "We like her," he said softly. There was a funny note in his voice that made me look at him. For a second, we stared right into each other's eyes.

I swallowed quickly and looked away. "What's her name?" I asked, then added stupidly, "your mother."

"Loretta. Loretta Jean."

"Jean's my middle name, too," I cried. I was excited that in at least one small way I was like this marvelous person.

"Has she been ill for long?" I asked him.

He didn't answer and I thought he hadn't heard. Then he said quietly, "No . . . not long at all."

He didn't say any more. It was pretty dark when we pulled up in front of my house. He took the bike out of the back of the truck and leaned it against the porch rail.

"Thank you," I told him.

"Sure, no problem."

He stood there for what seemed forever. I wanted so desperately to say something neat and charming and unforgettable. *Please God, give me the words*, I thought.

"Well . . ." he said finally. "See you tomorrow."

I managed to nod. He climbed back into the truck and left.

The kitchen light was on. I knew Mom would have supper ready. Even if she'd heard me tell her that I was going for a bike ride, she'd still be worried. She didn't like me out on the road after dark. When I walked into the house I was still so full of the Morgans' warmth and love that I had to smile. I'd never known a family like them. How I wished I could bring some of that warmth home.

Mom was standing by the stove. She turned and

slammed the spoon in her hand down on the counter, splattering spaghetti sauce all over the wall.

"Where have you been?" she shouted.

I opened my mouth to tell her, but the fury in her face stopped me. I shook my head. She wouldn't understand.

"Out." I whispered. Then I went upstairs to my room.

# CHAPTER

The way things were going, I wasn't the least bit surprised the next morning when Kim showed up at my back door wrapped in a bedsheet again. This time it was a purple and beige diagonal stripe, tied about the waist with a huge gold chain belt. Her feather and bead earrings hung clear to her shoulders, and she'd penciled her eyebrows in an upward sweep all the way to the hairline. She had hair again, thank goodness.

"Like it?" she asked, whirling so the sheet twisted around her ankles and almost tripped her.

"Yeah," I told her. "Sensational. All you need is a castanet in each hand and rings on your toes."

She grinned wickedly and pulled the sheet up to show me a huge green cut-glass emerald on one big toe.

Mom glanced out the door and I heard her gasp. I knew how she felt, but I'd die before I let her know that Kim's getup took my breath away, too.

As Kim and I started down the driveway, my thoughts went back to the night before. I'd gone to bed without any supper. Later on, Mom came upstairs. She didn't really apologize for yelling at me, but she stood in the doorway of my room for a long time without saying anything. It was almost as if she didn't know what to do or say. But only kids feel that way, don't they? Not grownups.

Finally she whispered, "P J, are you hungry?"

It was too dark to see. How did she know I shook my head? She walked close to my bed, and I think she might have kissed me, but I rolled over and pulled the covers up around my ears. Let *her* carry some of the guilt.

After awhile, she just touched my hair and left. I knew I wasn't being fair. She'd been mad and scared and upset when she'd yelled at me. Last night, I'd felt very self-righteous as I muttered to myself, "No one said life was supposed to be fair."

Today, it didn't make me feel any better at all. She was right, I guess. No one had ever promised me life would be fair. Even so, I'd expected a little more than what I was getting lately.

As we reached the top of the hill, Kim frowned at me.

"Why are you limping?" she asked. My knee was still stiff and sore and I walked a little like a sailor with a wooden leg.

"I fell on the blacktop with my bike last night," was all I said. Kim and I usually shared everything—but somehow I wasn't ready to tell her about Randy and his dad and especially about Loretta. Right now they were all mine and I didn't want to share them with anyone. Not yet.

The Morgans. That's what a family should be. Kind, soft-spoken—people who really cared about one another. No scary screaming matches where all the wrong words were shouted. Mr. and Ms. Morgan loved each other and showed it. It was plain to see how they both felt about Randy. I couldn't imagine any of them walking out—the way my dad had.

I could almost resign myself to the fact that he and Mom didn't love each other—almost. But what was wrong with me? Why didn't he care about me anymore?

"Deep thoughts today, Lib?" Kim asked. "I get nervous every time I see that look on your face." She winced and stopped to rub her foot. She'd made a pair of sandals by cutting the tops off a pair of tennis shoes and tying the soles to her feet with red laces. Walking seemed to be growing even trickier for her than for me and I had to slow down to match her small steps.

"Is it your dad?" she asked, wrinkling her nose as the laces tightened on her ankles.

Instantly, a lump formed in my throat. I couldn't speak and it made me furious. I gritted my teeth and nodded.

"I thought it might be. I saw his little friend in the car yesterday."

"He's moving to Florida with her." I managed to get it out without crying.

"Geez, that's tough. How soon?"

I couldn't answer.

"Oh no!" Kim said. I knew she'd figured it out right away. She was good at reading my mind. "Has he already left?"

A tear escaped from the corner of my eye and my nose started to run. I didn't want to cry, but whenever anyone showed me a little sympathy, I always fell apart.

Kim sighed. "I'm never getting married," she said. "And even if I do, I'm not going to have any kids. I'd never want to put a kid through what you and I . . . " She stopped walking and turned to look at me. Her face was serious. "Do you suppose they ever really wanted us? They treat us like . . . like . . . wasted space! Is that what we are? Just wasted space?"

She plopped her books down on the ground and sat on them, rubbing her foot.

"Rats! I'm going to have to think up a new design for shoes. These aren't going to work."

I saw the bus coming down the highway, all the red and yellow lights flashing merrily. Kim always said it looked like a yellow, 66-passenger Christmas tree.

"Come on," I told her. "We'll have to fix them on the bus."

We hobbled together to the corner just as Ms. James swung the door open. I could hear Brian's voice before I got one foot on the steps.

"Here they come, the creature from the black lagoon and the mummy." Even the grade-school kids laughed.

"Shut it up!" Ms. James had to shout to be heard. The laughter quieted to subdued giggles.

If only I could have died right there on the road so I didn't have to get on. Kim poked me in the back.

"Don't let that creep get your goat. Ignore him."

If I had had a goat, I would gladly have given it to Brian in exchange for leaving us alone. Step by step, every eye in the whole bus staring right at me, I managed to make it to our empty seat in the middle of the bus. No matter what Kim said, I'd given up all hope of ever sitting in the back. Now I just prayed we'd make it through the year sitting where we were. Next year, I would take driver's training and then I'd have my license. Maybe I could talk Mom into letting me get a car, if I paid for it myself. I tried to imagine how great it would be, pulling alongside the bus every morning in my own neat red convertible and sticking my tongue out at Brian as we went by.

"He only does that, you know, because he thinks it upsets you," Kim said, as she loosened the red laces.

"He's right," I couldn't keep my voice from quavering.

She hesitated. Then, still staring at her feet, she said, "I know how you can get him to leave you alone."

"How?" I whispered frantically. I was willing to try anything.

"Stop running around with me."

If someone had suddenly sent a shot of electricity through our bus seat, I couldn't have been more shocked. What was she talking about?

"Kim, I'd never do that!" I said it too loudly and everyone looked at me again. I ducked and lowered my voice. "I thought we were best friends."

Kim finally looked up at me. Her smile was shaky. The look in her eyes reminded me of the day we saw the mother fox and her babies. I was seeing inside her and it scared me. Kim was the strong one. Her self-confidence got us both through a lot of rough spots. She kept me from losing my grip on the edge of what she called my "pity-puddle." I didn't want to know she was scared too. I looked away.

"Well, it's true, isn't it?" she said softly.

"Probably," I said. "But it wouldn't be worth it."

Her smile turned a little crooked. Without a word, she went back to working on the red laces and tennis shoe soles. There was a funny set to her shoulders.

With all my bad qualities and even worse decisions, that was one thing that had never crossed my mind—shying away from Kim's friendship. Now that she'd brought it up, I knew she was right—Brian would never have noticed me if it hadn't been for her. I could have ridden the bus my whole life without a single person bothering to find out my name. In a way, it was a depressing thought. Almost—but not quite.

Kim poked me again. I hated it when she did that. I opened my mouth to tell her, and it remained open as I looked down the road.

"There's old Mizz-zzippi," she whispered. "And he's in trouble today."

Randy waited at the end of his driveway, one big hand shoved into the back pocket of a pair of jeans that were worn white. They'd been patched and repatched, as had the elbows of the red-checkered shirt he wore. One patch, just above his knee, was shaped like a heart. On the other leg there was a butterfly. The elbow patches were yellow circles with smile faces embroidered on them.

"Oh brother, can you believe that!" Brian was warming up before Ms. James even got the door open. "Look at the getup. This guy has got to be weird."

As Randy walked up the steps, Brian, or someone else, let out with a piercing wolf-whistle. Everyone laughed hysterically. My stomach was rolling. I could see the back of Ms. James' neck turning red. Randy quickly sat down in one of the front seats with the little kids.

Kim jabbed me with her elbow. "I think you'd do well to take him off your SOL list," she said with a little smile. "You need a guy with a few more guts."

I just stared at her.

"Hey, Douglas," someone behind us yelled. "A man for you at last."

Kim didn't even flinch. She stood up, turned, and leaned over the back of our seat. "Robert, you're just jealous 'cause I turned you down last week," she said loudly, batting her false eyelashes like mad.

Wild whoops and cat calls rang through the bus. I sank lower into my seat, but not before I'd seen Ms. James unlatch her seat belt and grab a handful of white conduct slips.

The shouting match continued until she marched to the back. Then it was so quiet I could hear the clicking noise as the outside warning lights flashed. Ms. James wrote out slips like a metermaid with an acre of illegally parked cars. An apologetic look flashed across her face as she handed one to Kim.

"I can't punish all the rest of them without including you, Kim," she said. "Sorry." Then she kind of looked at me as though she'd never seen me before, a puzzled expression on her face.

I smiled hopefully. She must have decided I hadn't been involved in the melee. She turned to face the back half of the bus.

"As you know," she said, her lips tight with anger, "these have to be signed by your parents and returned to me in the morning before you'll be allowed to ride the bus. No signed white slip—no ride. Understood?"

Everyone shuffled nervously and looked at one another. I heard tittering coming from the back but Ms. James didn't seem to hear, or maybe she was ignoring it. As she stalked back to her seat, I breathed a sigh of relief.

Randy turned around long enough to catch my attention. His mouth twitched in the barest suggestion of a smile. I hope I smiled back. I know my face turned its usual shade of pink.

Next to me, Kim giggled. "Won't this just frost old Brian's kazoo?" she said.

It was hard for me to understand why she loved trading verbal insults with Brian and his creepy friends. I could never think of anything brilliant and cutting to say.

"Will you get in trouble?" I asked Kim, looking at the hastily scribbled white slip. It consisted of a preprinted list of violations. Ms. James had circled "Loud and/or obnoxious talking" and "Refusal to cooperate with bus driver." Not only did it require a parent's signature, it also meant a trip to the principal's office and a detention.

Kim shook her head. "Think I'm crazy? I'll sign it myself. I make sure they don't ever see things like this," she said, that funny smirk twitching at the corner of her mouth. "It might upset them."

By "them" she meant her parents. I knew Kim was a complete mystery to them. Trouble on the bus was something concrete they could understand. They were likely to blow it all out of proportion.

Sometimes Kim was a little hard for me to understand, too. But after I thought it over for a few minutes, I realized Kim's smart reply had kept Brian from picking on Randy, and brought all the badgering down onto her own shoulders.

*Why did she do that?* I wondered. Randy didn't matter to her. It seemed as if she just wanted to be noticed. Was the attention that important to her? Any kind of attention?

We got off the bus at the high school. As we hurried toward the big entrance doors, I heard Brian yell Kim's name. Kim and I looked back. Brian gave us the finger. Kim laughed and stuck out her tongue. I turned around and pretended not to see.

All my life, I'd looked forward to my first year of high school. Now I wished I could have stayed in kindergarten.

# CHAPTER 8

On Saturday morning, I was wide awake long before dawn, wondering what had happened to all my resolutions for the new school year. All the good things I was going to do, such as make a few friends in the freshman class, and try to fit in. A little static from that creep, Brian, and I fled like a wounded goose.

All I wanted was to sit in the back of the school bus. Was that too much to ask?

After just a week of school, I could see how things were going to be for the rest of the year. Nothing had changed. Nothing was likely to change. Kim and I were going to be sitting in the middle-school seats until graduation, four long years away.

"Hang in there, Lib," Kim had told me firmly. "We'll be O.K. These are just *boys* . . . God's only mistake. Haven't I told you *she* forgot to give them brains?"

Usually, Kim's weird remarks cheer me up a lot, but right then it seemed my whole life was one big depressing nothing. Wasted space, just as Kim had said.

Believe me, I'd underestimated how I'd feel that first Saturday when Dad didn't come to pick me up.

How can a person be shivering with excitement and sick with dread all at the same time? It's how I'd felt all those other Saturday mornings, lying awake in the dark, knowing he was going to be there at eleven. I wanted with all my heart to be with him, but I also knew I'd invariably do something dumb and make the whole day stupid and boring for him.

Like the time at the super-elegant French restaurant, one of his favorite places, when I reached for the salt and spilled red wine on his cashmere sweater and tan slacks. He said not to worry, that it didn't matter, but he brought me home three hours early.

Or the day I was so nervous and ate too much popcorn and candy in the movie theater. I threw up all over the cream-colored velvet upholstery in his new sedan. I think I might have been home a little early that day, too.

But this Saturday was different from all the rest. He wasn't coming.

I stared at the dark ceiling of my bedroom for a long time, feeling empty inside. Not a feeling like when you're hungry, but a deep, echoing, hollowed-out feeling, like a blank-eyed Halloween pumpkin scooped clean. There was no nervous anticipation, no rushes of joy like during a rollercoaster ride. Nothing.

Long streamers of pink and gold flowed across the ceiling as the September sun inched up clear of the horizon. I tried to think of what I could do to pass the day that stretched endlessly before me. Absolutely nothing came to mind. I didn't want to get up—not ever.

My eyes traced the spider-web cracks marring the freshly painted plaster on the walls. I remembered the July day Mom and I had spent painting the little room.

The temperature and humidity were out of sight and I was grouchy to start with. I couldn't understand why she insisted we had to paint when the heat was so horrible. Also, I'd wanted a soft shade of blue and she insisted on green. I hate green!

Anyway, for once, Mom had been in a great mood. She sang and whistled all the while. She ran the roller up and down the wall as carefully as though she were painting the presidential suite.

Her cheerfulness was the most depressing thing of all.

"Why do we have to bother with this old dump?" I grouched.

"Because it has to be done," she said with a sigh. "Persimmona, you'll find out there are a good many things in life that will be very hard for you to do. But you'll do them, because if you don't, no one else will either."

I concentrated on the window trim. "If we'd stayed in our new house in town, we wouldn't have to keep patching on these crummy old walls."

She turned around and looked at me, the green paint dripping off the end of the roller onto the bare floor.

"We couldn't afford to stay there. You know that."

I swear I never would have said what I said if the weather hadn't been so hot and miserable and if I hadn't hated the color of the stupid paint so much.

"If you hadn't divorced Daddy, we could have stayed there." Even as the words rasped from between my lips, I was sorry and ashamed. It's too bad being sorry and ashamed has never yet shut me up when I start on one of my little tantrums.

I saw her body go rigid. "That's not fair," she said loudly.

"No one ever said life was supposed to be fair," I whined in an imitation of her voice.

"Persimmona!" she said in a tone that would have stopped a runaway freight train dead on the tracks. I knew I was asking big time for a slap across the face, but my mouth was in gear and I couldn't get it throttled down.

"Maybe he ran around with other women because you didn't love him enough." *Shutupshutup*, I thought.

She stepped toward me, her face white. I hoped she'd hit me. I deserved it. What was the matter with me, anyhow? I felt confused and sick to my stomach.

Then she did the very worst thing she could have done. She said softly, "A person does what she has to do, Persimmona. I hope someday you can understand that."

As I lay in bed on this Saturday morning, I hoped so too. The cracked ceiling became a blur as I blinked back tears.

The pink sunrise had turned to a golden glow inside my room. I heard Mom's bare feet pad softly down the stairs to the kitchen. After a few minutes, the smell of perking coffee drifted up to me. Why did coffee always smell so delicious and taste so bad?

"You can't just lie here until Sunday," I muttered. My body heard and obeyed. Barely. Out of a pile of clothes in the corner, I found my oldest pair of blue jeans. In my dresser, I scrounged for the crummiest sweatshirt I owned—to match my mood. Then I slipped my tennis shoes over my bare feet—because it drives Mom crazy when I go sockless, and that also matched my mood.

When I got to the top of the stairs, I heard her in the kitchen, humming softly to herself. I stood there for a long time. My fingers hurt from gripping the worn wooden railing. Finally I went back to my room, pulled my tennies off, put on a pair of clean socks, and jerked the shoes back on my feet. She probably wouldn't even notice.

She was sitting at the kitchen table with the paper and a cup of coffee, letting the sun wash over her shoulders. Her hair was tousled about her face like golden cotton candy. She would have looked like a little girl—if it hadn't been for the cigarette stuck in the corner of her mouth. Still she was so beautiful. Why couldn't I have inherited just a tiny bit of her beauty? Or even my dad's rugged good looks? How could the daughter of such handsome people be such a loser? Sometimes I wondered if I were adopted.

I paused in the doorway to swallow the lump in my throat. Then this brilliant idea began to creep into my head. Why did this day have to be such a downer? Maybe Mom and I could do something together. Maybe today could be the start of our very own little tradition—a mother-daughter Saturday.

Offhand, I couldn't think of a single activity we both liked, but I was sure we could work it out. A picnic? Bowling, maybe? I started to get excited. It was a chance for me to make it up to her—all the stupid hateful things I'd said lately.

I thought about the Morgans and how much they shared.

"Mom?" I said softly.

She jumped and almost dropped the paper. "P J, you scared me. I didn't hear you come down the stairs." She smiled and pulled the other chair out from the table. "Come sit with me. Do you want orange juice?"

I nodded and suddenly felt very shy. "I'll get it," I

said. I opened the refrigerator door and pretended to search for something. "Do you have anything planned for today?" I asked. "Want to do something?"

"Oh Honey, I'm sorry," she said. "Carl and I are going to a photography exhibit in Champaign. Carl got the tickets more than a month ago."

So much for the mother-daughter day.

"You're going to be with Creepy Carl all day?" I said. I blinked like mad to push back the rush of tears and pulled my head out of the refrigerator, grabbing the orange juice and slamming the door shut. As I walked to the cabinet to get a glass, she reached for me. I moved away. If she touched me, I knew I'd start to cry.

"Please don't call him that," she said. I could tell she was making a real effort to keep the anger out of her voice. "Persimmona, we made these plans a long time ago. I'm not used to having you around on Saturdays."

"I can go away if you like," I said irritably, splashing the juice into a plastic cup. Instantly I wanted to take the words back. Why had I said that? It wasn't what I wanted to say at all. I was constantly amazed at what came out of my mouth without passing through my brain first. I wanted to beat my head against the peeling wallpaper on the kitchen wall.

"My stars, Persimmona! Why are you such a brat!" Mom threw the paper on the floor and grabbed her coffee cup. She jumped up and stalked toward the living room, sloshing coffee on the worn linoleum tile as she went. At the doorway, she looked back over her shoulder and I saw tears shining in her eyes.

*Please*, I thought. *Don't do that to me. Don't heap the guilt on my back. I can't carry much more.*

It was no wonder Daddy had moved away from me.

My fingers suddenly went numb and I dropped the

cup of orange juice all over the floor. I stared at it for a long time. Was there no end to my dumbness?

Finally I mopped it up, but I left the coffee spots. She could wipe up her own mess.

After awhile, Mom appeared in the doorway again. "I've got an article to write," she said stiffly. "When Carl gets here, tell him I'm in my office."

She didn't pause long enough for me to tell her I was sorry. Or maybe I didn't try to say it fast enough.

Her office was just a tiny storage room underneath the stairs at the end of the downstairs hall. I heard the door slam with a crash that emphasized how upset she was with me.

I sighed. Experience told me I'd lost my chance. It was going to be hours—if not days—before she'd listen to any kind of apology.

I hung around the kitchen for an hour. After awhile, I turned on the TV, but the only thing on was cartoons, and they just depressed me even more.

The mailman pulled up to the mailbox and my stomach turned upside down. I knew it was too early to expect a letter from Florida, but I went running down the driveway anyway. I shuffled breathlessly through the stack of envelopes as I walked back to the house. A few bills, two rejection slips from publications where Mom had submitted manuscripts, and a lot of "Current Occupant" things that I threw unopened into the burn barrel next to the driveway.

The sun was warm on my back and I stopped before I went into the house. Across the road, the drying cornstalks rustled softly. A flock of blackbirds soared as one unit overhead, wheeling to change directions as if on a whim. Their harsh frantic cries drifted to me on the gentle breeze as they dropped like black hail into the cornfield.

I sniffed and squinted, looking up at the light blue September sky. The air was clean and sweet, with just a hint of the approaching fall. Perfect day for a bike ride.

And suddenly I knew where I wanted to ride to.

I wrote a note on the back of one of the envelopes, "Went to the Morgans," and ran upstairs to change my clothes.

# CHAPTER 9

I was a little more cautious this trip. It would be very embarrassing to show up on the Morgans' doorstep bleeding again. My knee was also just beginning to heal and the thought of falling on it gave me cold chills.

For some reason, I found myself out of breath as I pedaled. I couldn't decide if it was because I might get a chance to see Randy, or if I was eager to talk to Loretta, or if maybe I was just out of shape.

My bike tires bumped through the pot-holed driveway as I huffed and puffed up to the Morgans' back door. The yard was deserted, as was the lean-to garage where Mr. Morgan did his mechanic work. I was disappointed to see the red truck gone from its parking spot behind the house. Maybe Randy's dad had taken it, I thought hopefully as I leaned the bike against the tree in the backyard. Not that I disliked Mr. Morgan or anything, but I sure liked to look at Randy.

He was so quiet and sweet on the bus and Brian was giving him such a hard time. I wanted to put my arms around him—protect him from the world. My SOL syndrome, again. Why didn't I have the guts to stand up and tell Brian Lang what I thought of him? And while I was at it, tell him Kim and I—and Randy too—were going to sit in the back seats whether he liked it or not?

Because I was scared, that's why. Kim had it all wrong. It wasn't Randy who was the coward.

No one answered my knock. Finally I gathered the courage to open the door just a crack. "Hello?" I whispered. If Loretta was alone and resting, I didn't want to wake her.

"Come in, Sugar."

Her voice was so frail I barely heard her, but when I walked into the bedroom, her face was beaming. She was propped up against a pile of fluffy pillows. Her eyes were bright, her cheeks flushed and healthy looking. A stack of neatly folded clothes covered one corner of the bed and a pair of worn blue jeans lay across her lap. She put down the needle and thread she was holding.

"I called for you to come," she said breathlessly, leaning over to pull the chair closer to the bed. "I'm not very loud, don't you know. My, but I'm glad to see you, Persimmona. Sit right here and talk to me."

It made me feel good to have someone act so happy to see me. Everywhere else in the world, my presence seemed to be barely tolerated. I sank down into the chair and instantly felt as though I belonged there.

"Randy went with his dad on an errand. I insisted that he go. He stays around the place too much. A young boy needs to get out more. My but he'll be disappointed he missed you."

*Probably not*, I thought. *He'll probably be glad.* But I could feel my face get red anyway.

"How was your first week of school?" Loretta asked.

"School's O.K.," I said. Not a lie. School was only a

minor disaster. It was riding the bus that was intolerable. "Summer was too short, though."

"I know what you mean," Loretta said with a sigh. "Winter has a way of just sneaking up on a person." She picked up the needle she was trying to thread. "'Course, this winter will be a lot different for us. In Gulfport, the weather doesn't turn hard and mean as it does here."

"Gulfport," I said happily. "You lived in Gulfport." At last the mystery of "Guff-pote" was solved.

She nodded, peering intently at the thread and needle. Her smooth forehead wrinkled with concentration. I noticed her slender fingers shaking with the effort.

"Randy says there was some trouble on the bus this week," she murmured in an offhand way. "Says you and your friend Kim stood up for him."

I was speechless for a second. How much had Randy told her? I wondered if he'd finally said something about how Kim and I had made fun of his southern way of talking.

"No big deal," I said carefully. "Brian Lang makes trouble for anyone who's new. Kim knows how to get back at him, though."

"I'd like to meet your friend, Kim, Sugar. Bring her over if you can. She sounds . . . interesting."

I had to smile. Evidently, Randy had told her everything about Kim.

Loretta was still squinting at the needle. She frowned and sighed impatiently. "The holes in these needles get smaller every year."

"Here," I said. "I'll do it."

"Well, bless you," Loretta said, sighing again. "I

guess my eyesight is getting old right along with the rest of me."

"But you're not old at all," I said. She was so beautiful, so perfect. I couldn't believe she thought of herself as anything else.

I tied off the knot and handed the needle back. She gathered the jeans up and positioned a brightly flowered heart-shaped patch over one torn knee. I shuddered. I hoped they weren't Randy's.

"Patches are so ugly," she said as she sewed tiny, overlapping stitches around the heart. "I've always tried to brighten them up some. Ever since Randy was a toddler, I've made little hearts and smiles and flowers to patch his clothes. Randy always loved them."

Obviously Randy hadn't told her any differently, and I wouldn't either. Not for the world. Not when I could see the pleasure shining from her eyes as she stitched.

It seemed to be an awful effort for her to push the needle into the fabric and even more so to pull it back out. After a moment, she let the jeans fall into her lap. She smiled up at me.

"I'll rest a bit," she said, leaning back against the cushion of pillows. Her eyes closed.

She was lovely to look at. Her golden lashes rested like fine strands of silk on her almost transparent cheeks. Her white-blonde mane wisped about her face like a cloud of the angel hair Mom always puts under the Christmas tree. And her lips, even though they were pale, were perfectly shaped in a little bow, a touch of a smile tipping the corners up.

No one had ever mentioned why she was sick. I hoped it wouldn't be long before she was well and out of bed.

"Can I try it?" I asked. "The mending, I mean?" I

wasn't sure she was awake until the lashes fluttered open.

"Well, bless you," she murmured.

She gathered the jeans up and handed them to me, then sank back on the pillows as though the effort had exhausted her. After a moment, she turned her head to look at me.

"I don't mind so much being sick," she said. "Edward and Randy are good to help. That's the hardest part of it, I guess, that I can't *do* for them." The look in her eyes was a mixture of frustration and hopelessness.

"I'll be glad to help you," I said eagerly. "I've never tried mending before, but I'd love to help. With anything," I added. I bent to the sewing, carefully poking the needle into the jeans and then into the patch. After a few stitches, I stopped to inspect my work and my heart sank. The stitches ran off to the side a little and I could see the patch was going to have a wrinkle.

"Let's see, Sugar," Loretta asked.

Embarrassed, I reluctantly held the patch up for her to see.

"Why, that's just fine," she said with a wide smile. "Much better than I did when I first tried."

"Really?" I felt better than when I brought home an A on my report card. Right then, more than anything in the world, I wanted her approval. I wanted to do it right and listen to her praise. Carefully, I worked my way around the patch.

"Have you heard from your daddy?" Loretta asked. It was such an unexpected question, I jumped and jabbed the end of my finger. I shook my head.

"I'm not sure I ever will," I said. My insides started to

shake as they did the day he told me he was leaving.

Loretta's eyebrows lifted. "Well, of course you will, Sugar. You're his baby girl. He loves you, don't you know."

I dropped the sewing in my lap, biting my lip to hold back the tears that suddenly bubbled into the corners of my eyes. I couldn't remember anyone ever before saying the word *love* when they talked about Dad and me.

"Mom thinks he moved to get out of paying child support."

Loretta reached over and took my hand. "That may be true, for one reason or another," she said softly. "But it doesn't take away his being your daddy. You remember that and love him with all your heart."

"But what if he doesn't love me?" I cried.

"Persimmona," she said, and never had my name sounded so soft and beautiful. "Persimmona, love is meant to be given, don't you know? It's all the nicer when someone loves you back, but it's not essential. You have to give and give and give, and do you know what's so wonderful?" Her heavenly eyes became even more blue and transparent. I felt as if I were swimming in them.

"The more love you give," she whispered, "the more that will come back to you. Maybe not in a way you'll see right away. But one day, just as the robins come home in the spring, all the love you give will come back home to you."

Before I had time to dissolve into a puddle, the back door slammed. I heard footsteps running through the kitchen. Randy's father dashed into the bedroom. He was ghostly pale and wisps of hair hung about his

craggy face. I scrubbed the tears from my cheeks, but he was completely unaware of me.

Gulping for air, he knelt by the side of the bed. "Honey," he gasped. "That wreck of a truck . . . quit this side of Johnston. We couldn't get it . . . and it was getting so late . . . "

Loretta put her hand on his cheek with a touch so full of love that I was uncomfortable watching.

"Edward, it's fine," she told him softly. "I was all right. Why, I had such marvelous company I didn't even know you were gone so long."

Mr. Morgan looked up at me. There was so much gratitude on his face, it embarrassed me.

"Thank you," he whispered. "Per . . . Persimmona, is it?"

I nodded.

Before he could say more, Randy bolted into the room. I could tell he was making more of an effort than his father to keep his feelings under control, but his eyes were large and I could read the fear swirling in them.

He took in the whole scene at a glance and the tension drained out of him in one great breath. His huge hands unclenched and he bent over the bed to kiss his mother on the cheek.

"Why, you two worrywarts," Loretta said with a chuckle. "Don't you think your mama can take care of herself for a few minutes?" Her tone was gently chiding, but she was obviously loving every second of the attention.

I'd felt jealousy before—when Suzie first glanced at Harold, I turned green—but the jealousy that tightened around my throat as I watched the Morgans was different. What was it like . . . to be that close and happy? How I envied the warmth and love that flowed between them. Why did my own evenings have to be quick suppers and long shouting matches?

Randy and Mr. Morgan went to the kitchen to make hot chocolate for us.

"You all get along so well," I said. (I swear I did my best not to say "y'all.") "I wish Mom and I could sign a truce."

Loretta looked at me, her eyebrows raised into question marks.

"All we ever seem to do is fight," I explained. "We can't say two words to each other without starting World War Three."

Loretta's rich laughter surprised me.

"Why, Persimmona, Honey," she said. "We used to fuss and squabble with the best of 'em."

Her smile faded and her voice turned soft and wistful. "I miss it, don't you know."

I looked at her in amazement. Why in the world would she miss arguing with her family?

Later on, I understood. Right then, I thought she had to be a little bit crazy.

# CHAPTER 10

A week went by before Mom finally unbent enough to ask me about the Morgans. That's the longest she'd ever stayed mad. I'd never admit it to her, but I was starting to get worried. Did we have to fight *all* the time? I knew I'd acted like a brat, just as she had said, but couldn't she have been a little more understanding, too?

"They're Loretta and Ed Morgan," I told her. "They've moved into the house where Epplins used to live over on the next road. I met their son, Randy, on the bus."

Mom narrowed her eyes and peered at me. "Why are you speaking with that funny accent?" she asked.

My feathers ruffled immediately. "What funny accent?" I demanded loudly. But I could feel my face turning its usual shade of pink. I guess I did pick up a touch of Loretta's soft southern speech, but I insisted—at least to myself—that it was unintentional.

For once, Mom let it drop. "You've been spending a lot of time over there," she remarked casually. I knew she was making a real effort to talk to me without an argument.

"Loretta's been sick," I told her. "I play board games with her and Randy . . . things like that." Under my breath, I added, "She asked me to help her a little around the house."

This was, of course, a bare-faced lie. Loretta would never impose on anyone by asking for help. I'm strictly a volunteer, and I love every minute of it. But I knew Mom would get her nose out of joint if she found out how much work I was doing at the Morgans'. For a second, I felt guilty about not feeling guilty. I made a silent vow to do a little more work around my own house. After all, Mom worked all day and half the night.

"Well," Mom said indignantly. "I'd like to know her secret. I work all day and half the night and I can't get you to do the least little thing around here."

So much for not arguing.

"I do a lot of work here," I said, just as indignantly. "And let me tell you, Loretta shows a lot more appreciation."

"Tell me why I should have to thank you for cleaning up your own room!" Mom shouted.

The conversation went downhill from there, right to the place where Mom invited me to pack my clothes and move in with the Morgans for good, although not in those exact words. She punctuated the statement, as she always does, by slamming her office door.

By then I was crying and screaming rash threats of my own. I even went as far as to run upstairs and pull my suitcase out from under the bed, but my hands were shaking so hard I couldn't open the latch. By the time I got it open, I'd calmed down enough to know I really didn't want to find a new place to live.

What I wanted was to get out for a few hours. I

grabbed my sweater and had my hand on the back door when the phone rang. It was Kim.

"How about coming over for awhile?" she asked. "Maybe you can straighten out how I feel about algebra." There was a lot of shouting going on in the background and I could barely hear her. I didn't have to ask what it was. I recognized some of the words.

"I'm going over to the Morgans'," I told her.

"Oh." was all she said.

"Listen, why don't you go with me? Loretta wants to meet you."

"I don't know . . . " her voice was doubtful. The noise behind her was getting louder.

"Come on, Kim. We'll walk over. It's quiet out there."

Over the phone, I heard the crash of breaking glass. Kim's voice was just a whisper.

"All right," she said. "Wait for me."

I put on my sweater and slipped out the back door without bothering to tell Mom I was going. *Let her worry*, I thought. As if she'd even notice I was gone!

I sat on the cool cement steps and watched the last half of the sun bleed into the fields behind the house. Down the road, the west windows on Kim's house shimmered with gold, then crimson and purple, then darkness.

Just the night quiet made me feel better. I began to wish I had it in me to go back inside and make up with Mom.

I became aware of a figure walking toward me. Something cold ran across the back of my neck. It wasn't Kim. I stood up and put my hand on the screen door.

"Hello?" I called. Even to me, my voice sounded a little shaky.

"Just me, Lib," a voice called back. "Please don't panic. I can't stand any more of that tonight."

It *was* Kim, but . . .

I peered at her through the dark. When she finally stood in front of me, I could see why I hadn't recognized her. She was wearing a beat-up sweatshirt—probably her dad's—and a pair of regular jeans. There were honest-to-goodness sandals on her feet, and her hair was swept back in a plain ponytail. Her face was absolutely clean of makeup. I couldn't believe it.

I didn't realize how long I'd been staring until she spoke.

"Have I turned green or something?"

"Almost," I said. "What happened to the protest against the religious harassment of the Persian Magi?"

Just a ghost of a smile touched her lips as she shrugged.

"After weeks of fasting, praying, soul-searching, and sacrificial offering, I've been informed by the great god Rha that they can get along without me . . . "

She turned away from me as she spoke and I didn't quite hear the end of the sentence, but I was pretty sure she added, "like everyone else."

I didn't ask any questions as we walked down the blacktop road; for the same reason she didn't ask me anything. Both of us knew and understood that we were each licking wounds too fresh to expose. Maybe later we could share the pain.

That was one of the best things about our friendship. We didn't have to blubber about our problems all the time. The understanding between us was so deep, we were comfortable with each other without saying a word.

"Do you know them really well?"

We'd walked for a long time in silence and Kim's question startled me. I stared at her dumbly.

"The Morgans," she explained carefully as though she were talking to a fencepost. "Have you gotten to know them pretty well?"

I nodded. "I try to help around the house a little, but I spend a lot of time just talking to Loretta," I told her. "She wants me there more to talk to than to help."

"What's Randy like? Still on your SOL list to be rescued?"

I was glad it was finally dark so she couldn't read the emotions on my face. I didn't want her to know what a complete fool I was over Randy.

"He's going to be pretty hard to convince that he needs to be rescued," I said. "He's a neat guy already. I sure haven't had to worry about fighting him off, though. Once in awhile, he remembers to say 'Hi, Pu-u-r-rsimmona.'" I smiled to myself as I thought about Randy's beautiful drawl. "That's about as intimate as we get."

I couldn't see Kim's face. I heard her sigh. It was a kind of sad sound. She didn't say any more until we walked into the Morgans' back yard. Yellow light streamed through the glass in the door. I could hear soft voices from within. Just being near them made me feel better.

"Maybe I'll wait out here," Kim whispered.

"Come on, Kim," I argued. "Loretta asked me to bring you. She'll be tickled to death."

Kim laughed, a strange harsh sound I'd never heard before. It gave me goosebumps.

"Lib," she said. "You're really something."

Before I could try to figure out what she meant, the back door swung open. Mr. Morgan looked down at us, his face stretched in a broad welcoming smile.

"I thought I heard voices out here. Come in, ladies. Please come in and join us." He stepped back and executed a low sweeping bow.

Kim put her hand over her mouth and giggled. It sounded more like the old Kim. As we walked into the brightly lighted kitchen, I felt as if things were right in my life, too. Mr. Morgan took us into the bedroom. He sat down in a large, overstuffed chair in a shadowed corner.

Loretta was sitting up, stitching a bit of red material onto the knee of a pair of coveralls. Kim looked at the rose-shaped patch and then at me, her eyes wide, but she didn't say a word.

"Oh my, isn't this just the nicest surprise?" Loretta beamed at us. "You brought your friend, Kim." She held out both hands and, after a second's hesitation, Kim took them in her own. I felt just the smallest twinge of jealousy. I pretended not to notice and picked up the shirt I'd been working on the day before.

It was Randy's shirt, of course. I especially enjoyed patching his clothes. After all, if I couldn't hold him . . .

You get the idea.

Sometimes, without being asked, I washed dishes or vacuumed the floor. I even tried to scrub the crust of grease off the stove. It wasn't immaculate, but it looked a lot better. Loretta was so grateful. I loved doing it. I would have done anything for her.

I seated myself in the rocking chair next to the bed and pretended to be completely engrossed in sewing the flower-shaped patch onto the elbow of the shirt.

But I didn't miss a word between Kim and Loretta.

"Well, I do declare," Loretta said. "Are all the girls in this neighborhood as pretty as you two? Must be the air around here."

I was shocked when I peeked up through my eyelashes and saw Kim's face redden. It was the first time in my whole life that I'd seen her at a loss for words.

Loretta didn't give her time to be embarrassed. "Come on now, Sweetheart," she said, patting the chair on the other side of her bed. "Sit down here and tell me all about yourself."

Deep inside, I was glad Loretta hadn't called Kim "Sugar." I wanted the name to be reserved just for me.

Kim sat. With some gentle prodding, she told Loretta a few general facts about herself and her family, but I could tell she was getting more nervous with every word.

When Randy stuck his head in the door, she clammed up like a frightened sparrow. Randy glanced around the room.

"I thought I heard company," he said, grinning. "Hi, Persimmona."

He looked at Kim and I saw her face go pale. She scrunched a little lower into the chair. I wondered what in the world could be wrong with her. I'd never seen her react to anybody that way.

"Hi, Kim," Randy said quietly.

"Hi, yourself, Randy," she answered, but there was none of the usual bravado in her voice. She jumped to her feet and turned to me.

"I've got to get home, Lib," she said breathlessly. "Nice to meet you," she said to the Morgans as she headed for the back door.

84

She was gone before I could say anything to stop her. No one in the room said a word.

"Goodness," Loretta finally whispered. I was stunned to see tears in her eyes. For an instant, I felt a murderous hate for Kim. I would have killed *anyone* who hurt Loretta's feelings.

Then reason set in. Kim was my *best friend.* Sometimes she did things that astounded me right down to my toes, but there wasn't a speck of deliberate meanness in her.

"She didn't mean to be rude," I cried out. "She wouldn't hurt anyone's feelings for the world."

I saw Loretta and Randy look at each other.

"Persimmona, Sugar," Loretta said. "I know she wouldn't. It just hurts me that I can see so much pain inside of her." She took my hand. "Go after her. She needs a friend right now more than anything else. Kim *needs* you, don't you know?"

I didn't know what she was talking about. Of all the people I knew and cared about, Kim seemed the most able to handle whatever came along. She was my rock—the one who gave me strength to cope with my own problems.

But Loretta had asked me to do something, and I couldn't deny her anything.

"Right," I said, tossing the mending into the pile on the table and bolting for the door. "See you later."

I had to run a long way to catch up to Kim. She didn't act too glad to see me, but it was funny. All the way home, I had the feeling she wanted to tell me something.

If only I'd just asked what was wrong, maybe the rest of it would have been different.

# CHAPTER 11

It seemed to me in the weeks that followed that my whole life was kind of summed up by the cold and rainy, endless days. The oaks around our house had barely changed into their fall plummage before the gloom turned the leaves dark. Then an angry November wind stripped the leaves from the branches and left them in soggy brown heaps on the ground. The weather matched my mood.

Mom hadn't said a whole lot to me since the *big fight*. Nothing at all, in fact. We ignored each other as much as possible. I guess that's one way to stop fighting, but it didn't make me feel a bit better.

Kim was stranger than ever—strange because she was dressing as normal people do. *Normal* was not an adjective I would ever have used to describe Kim—at least not until lately. I worried about her.

And to top it off, not a word had filtered back to me from Florida. I figured Dad was having such a good time swimming, and sailing and fishing and chasing beautiful women in bathing suits, that his only daughter had completely slipped his mind. But then, I guess I slip easily from *anyone's* mind.

The only bright hours in my life were those spent at the Morgans'. I went over every chance I got, without making Mom madder than she already was. Since she was so uptight about my being friends with the Morgans, I usually waited until she went to class or was out on a date. Thank you, Creepy Carl.

The Morgans' house felt like a real home. I don't mean to say the place was neat and clean and smelled like fresh baked bread all the time. It was just that Loretta and Randy and his dad weren't afraid to talk and laugh and touch. Once I saw Randy hug his dad and kiss him on the cheek. For a second, I was embarrassed. It was the first time I'd ever seen two men do that. Then when I thought about it for a minute, it made me feel good.

One night, when I was sewing a patch onto a pair of jeans, I told Loretta how I felt. She laughed softly.

"To out and out show people you love them is a skill that a lot of folk aren't born with, Sugar. Me . . . I knew all along God put me here to share all the love I could . . . , but Randy and Edward . . . they had to learn."

"But how do you learn?" I asked. I wished I'd been able to hug my own dad. I couldn't even imagine hugging my mom. She'd probably be more embarrassed than I would be.

Loretta put the mending down in her lap and stared at me very seriously. "You can't wait for the other person," she said. "You have to be the one who reaches out . . . the one who takes the first step . . . even though it also makes you the one most likely to be hurt."

I felt the corners of my eyes stinging as I thought about the letter from my dad that had never arrived. But before I could ask any more, Randy came in with a huge bowl of popcorn.

"Well, I've got enough for me," he said with a grin. "What are the rest of you going to eat?"

Mr. Morgan pretended to wrestle the bowl from Randy's grasp, and they ended up breathless and laughing, popcorn all over the floor. While Mr. Morgan went back to the kitchen to pop more, Randy set up the Scrabble game on the bed. Loretta won the first move. She spelled L-O-V-E across the center star. She winked at me and I felt warm and close and a part of them.

The rest of the evening was spent laughing over nonsense words that we all insisted were "right there in the dictionary." But as always the fun had to end and I had to go home. Our house seemed colder each time I returned—more empty and bare.

Just as bare as the cornfields were now, the broken stalks poking up here and there in jagged rows. It seemed strange to be able to see clear across the field to Kim's yard. In July, when the corn was at its tallest, only the upper windows of her house were visible, even from my room. Now, in the mornings while I waited on our backstep, I could see her as she left her front door. I had a funny feeling she might have walked right on by my house if I hadn't been out there to catch her.

I wished I had the nerve to just come right out and say, Hey Kim, what's *wrong*? I could tell something was. It wasn't that all of a sudden she was wearing normal clothes. Worse than normal, really; blouses that were badly ironed, and skirts with the hem hanging; scuffed shoes and pastel socks that needed to be washed. It was more that she didn't care at all. About anything.

On a gloomy November afternoon, I found out what I'd wanted to know. Funny. It was everything that I had *never* wanted to know, too.

We were sitting in our usual middle-school seats on the bus. Even Kim seemed to have admitted defeat about that. She stared silently out the window. Her eyes were kind of dull and surrounded by purple circles dark enough to be bruises.

Brian had tried to bait her once or twice that afternoon. After a few more nasty remarks directed at Randy were also ignored, he gave up. It seemed as if the whole bus was in a slump.

The little kids around Kim and me were grouchy and argued all the time. They called one another names. The resentful looks we got spoke volumes. They wanted us out of their section as badly as we wanted to get out.

"I'm going over to the Morgans' this afternoon," I whispered.

Kim shrugged. "So what else is new?" she said, still looking out the window.

"So why don't you go with me? Loretta would love to have you visit."

"No, I don't think so," Kim said. There was a funny smile on her face. "I can't handle all that goodness."

"Come on," I pleaded. It sort of irritated me when she subtly slammed the Morgans like that. "You don't have anything else to do."

"Sure she does. Lots of things," a sarcastic voice from the seat behind us said.

I stiffened with surprise. It was Rich Lawson, a senior who was such a low-life that even Brian Lang avoided him. He'd never spoken to Kim or me before, and I hoped fervently that this was the first and last time. He leaned forward on the back of our seat. His zit-covered face was close to my ear, his breath rotten with the stench of cigarettes and the scum on his unbrushed teeth. I wanted to gag.

"Isn't that right, Kimmy?" he whispered.

I had to turn my head away and hold my breath to keep from throwing up. When I looked back, I saw that Kim's face had turned pasty white.

"What's he talking about?" I whispered. There was a quivering knot in the pit of my stomach.

A muscle twitched at the corner of Kim's mouth, but she didn't look at me.

"Kim?" I was beginning to feel scared.

"How about it, Kimmy?" the vile voice from behind us sneered. "How about a date with me tonight? You aren't going to waste yourself with Ronnie Wilson, are you?"

The bus slowed for our corner. Kim jumped up and climbed over me as though the seat were on fire. She was halfway down the aisle before the bus stopped. I followed her, my mind whirling. Behind me, Rich's slimy laughter grated at my skin like sandpaper.

I stumbled down the steps and ran after Kim. She was halfway up the hill, her books clutched tightly to her chest. I caught her by the arm and pulled her to a stop. Still, she wouldn't look at me.

"Tell me," I gasped. "Tell me he didn't mean what I think he meant."

When she finally raised her head, her eyes had a flat, lifeless expression. I was looking at someone I didn't know.

"It's one way of sitting in the back seat, isn't it?" she said with a weak smile.

I couldn't answer. The look on her face told me it was true.

Still, I couldn't believe it. Not Kim. Not my best friend, who was as ignorant about the ways of men as I was, and just as scared to learn. Not Kim—please God!

"Why?" I whispered. I didn't even care that tears were sliding down my face. "And with Ronnie Wilson! What a creep!"

Bright pink patches glowed on Kim's cheeks. "I can't hang around that stupid house night after night and listen to *them* fight," she said. "And I can only sit in the library just so long. I needed someone, Libby. A warm body."

She lifted her chin and turned around, trudging up the hill.

I didn't know what to say or do.

"What about me?" I cried. "Why didn't you come to me? Don't I count? We could have talked about it."

She stopped walking and shook her head slowly without turning. "I tried, Lib, really. But you spend all your time with Randy and his mother."

"You could have come with me," I said. "I asked you . . . "

"Get off it, Lib! You didn't want me there. Not any more than I'm wanted at home. Don't you think I can tell?"

I almost said "That's not fair." But I could imagine Mom saying the same thing, and I knew exactly what Kim's thoughts would be.

Kim continued up the road with slow, even steps. I didn't have anything else to say that would matter.

"Kim," I shouted. "At least can't you think of how your mom and dad will feel if they find out?"

She whirled around, her long hair sweeping across

her face. The look in her eye took my breath away. I cringed as she stepped back toward me.

"Mom and Dad?" she said quietly. "It'd be great if they find out. Maybe I'll even tell them about it. Maybe I'll get pregnant and then tell them."

I knew my mouth was hanging open with amazement. I'd never heard Kim talk this way. "It'll kill them, Kim," I whispered.

"They won't care," she said bitterly. "They don't care about me. Nothing matters to them. They're too busy getting a divorce." She shut her eyes tight and screamed it. "They're getting a divorce!" Her face twisted into the shattered mask of a person I didn't recognize.

"Oh Kim," I said. "I'm sorry." I reached out for her. She pushed my hand away.

"I tried to tell you that night a week ago, but you were too busy with your precious Morgans!"

My head was pounding. Loretta's words were running over and over in my mind. "It hurts me to see the pain in her. She needs you. She needs a friend, don't you know." I was supposed to be Kim's best friend, but Loretta had seen that something was wrong with her long before I even suspected.

"I know how you feel, Kim," I cried with her. "I went through it, too. It's not the end of the world. It won't do any good to try to punish them like this."

"How can you know how I feel?" Kim's voice rose to a shriek. "You . . . you wander around like Wendy in your own little Never Never Land. Well, you don't have to hang around with me because you feel sorry for me. I don't think you really care about anyone but yourself."

"That's not true," I said.

"Oh yes it is!" she hissed. "All you care about is

yourself and your sweet little Loretta. And I've got news for you . . . she moved here to see the doctor Mom works for . . . Loretta's going to die!"

My world stopped. Even the wind was still. I couldn't feel my body. Nothing would move. My mouth wouldn't open.

Kim's eyes widened with anguish as her face crumpled into lines and shadows.

"I'm sorry," she whispered. "I'm . . . " She whirled and fled down the gravel, leaving me frozen.

I heard someone saying "No!" over and over. The voice was thin and scratchy and frightened. It was a long time before I figured out it was my own. My arms were numb and my books and folders slid out of my grasp into the ditch. Papers fluttered across the gravel. My feet moved with a will of their own, back to the corner, down the blacktop. Running. Running.

It wasn't true. I knew it wasn't true. She was too beautiful, too kind and good. She gave nothing but love to the world.

And she was going to die.

I don't know how I ran all the way from my corner to the Morgan place. Later, I couldn't remember doing it. What was imprinted on my memory forever was the look on Randy's face when I staggered up the driveway.

He was raking the yard, piling the dead leaves into huge mounds along the edge of the road. At first, he smiled at me. I must have looked pretty dumb running down the road in my denim skirt and little red pumps.

Then his smile disappeared. He dropped the rake and took a step toward me. I was gasping for breath. I stood in front of him for what seemed like forever before I could say anything.

In all that time, he didn't say one word. I knew the question I was going to ask was written all over my face.

Randy reached out and touched me.

"It's true, isn't it," I whispered. "She's not going to get well."

His big hand dropped helplessly to his side. He nodded.

The thing in the pit of my stomach slithered up around my heart and squeezed like a python.

"Why didn't you tell me!" I cried.

He gazed off over my shoulder. I saw him swallow as though something was stuck in his throat.

"She didn't want us to tell you," he said. "She didn't want to upset you, Persimmona."

"Upset me!" I shouted. "No one thought I might be upset if I came skipping over here one day and she . . . ?" I couldn't finish the thought. Anger was the only defense I had against the pain. I remembered the look between him and Loretta the night I'd brought Kim over.

"You knew about Kim, too." I made a statement of fact. Of course he knew. That's why Kim was so uncomfortable around him. The pieces were falling together—crumbling in a little heap around my feet.

Randy nodded again. "Those kind of guys talk. I heard about it along with everyone else in the locker room."

*Oh no*, I thought. Poor Kim was being discussed in the boys' locker room.

"And you didn't tell me because you thought it might upset me, right?" By this time, tears were staining the front of my good blouse.

"She's your best friend. I thought she ought to tell

you herself." He put his hands on his hips and stared at the ground. "If I thought wrong, I'm sorry."

I couldn't think of anything else to say. Nothing that mattered. Right then, the absurdity of my anger didn't cross my mind—his mother was dying and I was *mad* at him.

"Persimmona, why don't you go and talk to Mama?" he said softly. The anger left me like air out of a burst balloon. My knees quivered. I shook my head.

"I can't," I said. "I can't." But even as I spoke, I followed him toward the house.

All the other times I'd walked in the back door, it'd been like escaping to another world. A world of warmth and love. It didn't belong to me, but I was allowed to share in it, and it kept me coming back.

Now I stood in that doorway and knew I never wanted to go in there ever again.

Was I like Kim said? Was I Wendy trying my best to stay in Peter Pan's world where I would never have to grow up? Where everything would stay the same forever?

"Persimmona, Sugar, what's wrong?" Loretta held out her arms to me. I looked into her beautiful pale blue eyes and saw the concern and love. I ached with the need to have her hold me and tell me everything would be all right.

But it wasn't going to be all right, not ever again. I whirled and fled back through the kitchen. Randy stood aside and let me by without a word. I felt his gaze following me but I didn't turn around.

I ran until the little red pumps rubbed blisters on my heels. When I finally stumbled up to my back door, the blisters were raw and bloody. But they weren't the reason I was crying.

# CHAPTER 12

It's a funny thing about nightmares—when you first wake up, they're still so sharp in your mind that there's often a sick feeling deep in your stomach. After awhile, the edges blur. The whole thing begins to look stupid. Finally it disappears. You can't even remember what the dream was about and you feel a little embarrassed that it scared you so badly to begin with.

When I woke up the next morning, I kept my eyes tightly shut. I pulled the covers over my head and gave the worst nightmare of my life a chance to fade away.

But this morning the images just became more clear and painful. I had to keep swallowing to hold down the lump in my throat.

After awhile, I couldn't ignore the sounds Mom was making downstairs as she got ready for work. The coffee pot bubbled, the refrigerator opened and shut, papers rustled—just an ordinary day.

For her.

I could feel the whole side of my face twitching as I clenched my teeth to keep from crying. I didn't want to get up. I wanted to live and die right here—under the old brown comforter.

How could I get on the school bus? The dread was a cold stone in my stomach. How could I face Randy? It was *his* mother who was dying. What could I say to him? And Kim. I felt guilty as though what was happening to her were *my* fault. I felt angry, too. Betrayed.

Loretta had betrayed me. She'd let me love her and need her. She was leaving me.

I couldn't think about it anymore. I threw the comforter away from me, trying to think of an excuse for missing school that would get by Mom. After examining my face in the bathroom mirror, I decided I looked too healthy to plead sickness. How could that be when I felt so awful inside?

Outside my window, a gray-black mist filled the air, so heavy it dripped from the leafless branches of the oaks. *A typical nightmare day*, I thought dismally.

"Persimmona?" Mom's voice floated up the stairs. "Are you ready for school yet? I have to leave in just a few minutes."

"I'm almost ready," I yelled back as I sat on the edge of the bed in my pajamas. I coughed several times, as loud as I could. Then I walked downstairs.

"Persimmona Jean!" Mom's voice was shocked. "You haven't even started to get dressed yet. The bus is going to be here in twenty minutes."

The thought made my stomach turn upside down. For that one second, I must have really looked sick. Mom's eyes widened.

"Do you feel all right?" she asked.

I shook my head. "No, I don't," I told her. It was true. I felt so bad right then I wanted to cry. I didn't even have to pretend.

Mom touched my face and stared into my eyes with

the special look she has that I hardly ever see nowadays. Then I really did start to cry.

"Honey, what's the matter? Do you hurt somewhere?"

If she only knew how bad I hurt . . .

I nodded. I had to tell her. "It's Loretta Morgan," I whispered. "She's sick, Mom. She's going to die."

A funny look swept across Mom's face. She hesitated for a second, then put her arms around me. "Oh, Honey, how terrible! I'd heard rumors, but I thought maybe . . . "

My whole body went stiff. I jerked away from her. "You knew?" I croaked. I couldn't keep my voice from quivering.

Mom nodded. She reached out to touch me.

"And you didn't tell me?" I said loudly, turning my back to her. I couldn't help myself. My insides were shaking. I started to shout. "Am I the only one in the whole world who didn't know?"

"I thought it might be just a rumor," she said. "I guess I thought the Morgans would tell you if it was true and they wanted you to know."

I couldn't believe it! "What am I, a carrot? Can't anyone tell me anything?"

I knew I was screaming and crying at the same time, but I couldn't turn it off. "I'm not a baby! I have a right to be included!"

It scared me, the way sobs kept bubbling up my throat, almost choking me. Hard as I tried, I couldn't stop them. I plopped down in one of the shaky kitchen chairs. It wobbled under me, but it was still safer than my legs.

"Look, I'm sorry about Loretta Morgan," Mom said quietly. "It's a terrible thing for the family . . . but you've got to realize that life has to go on, Persimmona. You need to understand . . . "

"Understand!" I sobbed. "How can I understand? She's so kind and so good. Why did it happen to her? Why is she the one who has to die?"

The expression on Mom's face shifted to something that made her look old and tired. She ground her cigarette out in her coffee cup and spoke without looking up at me. "Would you be this upset if it were me instead of her, Persimmona?"

My sobs dried up like a sponge in the desert. Why would she say that? It wasn't the same at all.

"That's not fair," I whispered. My voice quavered and I couldn't hold it steady.

Mom just looked at me. Deliberately, she took another cigarette from her purse on the counter, lit it, and took a long drag. She gathered her papers and tucked the purse under her arm, then tipped her chin up and blew smoke toward the ceiling.

"I have a date with Carl tonight," she said. "I won't be home to fix supper." She walked out the door. In a moment, I heard the green Frog sputter to life. Gravel clattered against the side of the house as the car shot down the driveway.

I don't remember getting ready for school. I just knew I couldn't spend the whole day in the house alone. When I ran down the road to the top of the hill, the bus was just pulling away from the corner. Clutching my books with one hand, I waved frantically with the other. The brake lights went on and the bus screeched to a stop. When I finally climbed up the steps, all out of breath, Ms. James frowned at me, but I didn't have the heart to even be embarrassed.

I stopped at the first seat and glanced around.

Everyone was looking at me, everyone but Kim. She had turned away and pretended to be staring out the window.

"Oooh my, come back and sit with us, P-u-u-rsim-mona!" A voice from the back seats tried to imitate Randy's beautiful southern drawl. It sounded ugly. Filthy. I sat down in the front seat with two kindergarteners.

When Randy got on the bus, I pretended to be reading my history book. His hip brushed against my elbow and I felt my face turn red. Had he done it on purpose? I couldn't decide, but I knew I couldn't talk to him right now. I was scared that, if I opened my mouth, weird words were going to come flying out.

So we went to school, Kim, Randy, and I, three little islands in a giant sea of gloom. They needed me, and Loretta needed me too. Why couldn't I be strong? Why couldn't I do what I had to do?

Instead, I shut my eyes and floated away—Wendy all the way. But didn't Wendy finally make the decision to go back and grow up? Or was that Tinker Bell? I didn't want to think about it anymore. Even my eyes hurt.

When we pulled into the parking lot, the old, gray-stone school looked cold and uninviting. I knew it held no answers for me. I wished I'd stayed home. Judging by the mood Mom was in when she left home, I decided she probably wouldn't have cared *what* I did.

As the day dragged on, my suspicions were confirmed; I should have stayed home. I must have had a blank look on my face. My English teacher—the vulture—stopped right in the middle of a sentence and pointed at me.

"What do you think about that, Persimmona?"

I had no idea what she'd been saying. Sweat popped out on my forehead as I tried to gather my thoughts.

"Ah . . . I . . . ," I mumbled. I cleared my throat a few times. I heard muffled giggles. Still the vulture stared accusingly at me, daring me. Finally I said it. "I wasn't listening."

"What?" she said loudly and triumphantly.

I jumped up, banging my knee on the desk. "I wasn't listening," I shouted.

The giggles stopped. Some of the kids looked at me as if I were weird. Who cared! I was numb.

The vulture blinked rapidly several times. Then she did something very strange. She walked over and put her hand on my shoulder. It felt warm and soft and not like a talon at all.

"Persimmona," she said quietly. "Do you feel all right? Would you like to go to the nurse's office and lie down for awhile?"

I just stared at her dumbly. Finally she scribbled out a pass and sent me out the door. I fled into the cool dimness of the hall.

Never had the founding fathers stared down from the pukey green walls so accusingly. The stern eyes seemed to blame me for everything that was going wrong.

But I didn't *do* anything, I cried silently. No, of course not. Nothing at all. I was making absolutely no effort to make anyone feel better. Not even me.

I couldn't face all the questions in the nurse's office. I sat in a dark corner until the next bell rang.

Somehow I struggled through the rest of the day. After an hour of stupid impressionistic dancing in gym class, I walked up to the wall chart in the locker room and penciled an M after my name. I didn't care who watched. Then I changed my clothes and sat in a corner of the auditorium until the last bell rang.

Kim walked right by me on the bus. She went to the back and sat with Rich Lawson, then looked to see if I was watching. I was—just long enough to see Rich put his arm across the back of the seat. At that point, I had to turn around to keep from throwing up.

My chest hurt. Once, Kim would have told me it was my SOL syndrome getting the best of me again. Now the joke seemed silly and something from long before, when I was a little kid.

At our corner, I stayed in my seat until Kim was out the door and starting up the hill. When I followed, I made sure my steps were slower than hers. I was afraid to talk to her. I didn't know what to say or what to do.

She was already in her front yard when I reached my mailbox. I watched until she opened the front door and went inside. She didn't look back.

There was a letter in the mailbox with a Florida postmark. My fingers were shaking so hard I wrinkled the envelope as I ran into the house and upstairs to my room. I threw my books onto the bed and opened the flap, being careful not to tear the single sheet of paper.

"Hi," the letter began. "How are you?"

I stopped reading. My hands felt like claws. I crumpled the paper into a ball and threw it into the wastebasket next to the bed.

"Fine," I muttered. "And how are *you?*"

I went downstairs and sat on the backsteps.

Night came slowly, creeping into the yard and over the naked oaks like a frightened animal. Everything around me was cold and wet and silent. I couldn't go back into the darkened house.

A car roared by, a rusty old dump with a crumpled fender and almost no muffler. It was packed with guys and girls, all of them laughing and shouting. The car slid to a stop in Kim's driveway. I saw the front door of the house open. The inside light of the car went on as someone opened the door and crawled in. In a second, the old heap rumbled back down the road, spraying gravel into our yard. A beer can shot out of an opened window and clattered down our driveway almost to my feet.

After awhile, because there was nothing else that I knew of to do, I got up and walked down the road toward the Morgans'.

# CHAPTER          13

The old farmhouse was faded and peeling and needed a new roof. I'd never noticed before. Light streamed out into the darkness through windows cracked and stained with age. But until yesterday, this place had been a magic kingdom. More so than even Walt Disney could have imagined, because the magic in it was not plastic and wires and bright-colored lights. The magic glowed from the fairy queen.

And now the queen was going to die. She and the magic would be gone from my life forever. I no longer felt safe and protected.

Randy didn't say a word when he let me in the door. Avoiding his eyes, I walked quickly by him. He and his father stood back in the shadows of the room and let me find my own way.

I couldn't look at her. I glanced from the ceiling to the floor to the stack of mending on the table next to her. Everywhere but into the eyes of the beautiful face I knew so well.

"Persimmona," she said softly. Her voice flowed about me like a soft spring breeze. "Come sit with me, Sugar."

I sat on the chair next to the bed and folded my hands tightly in my lap, staring at them intently. I didn't know what to do or say.

"I'm sorry, Sugar," she whispered. "I'm sorry I'm going to leave you. I know how it hurt when your daddy left." She sighed. "Guess I shouldn't have let you get so near . . ."

I was horrified. I looked at her at last, feeling tears stinging the corners of my eyes.

"No!" I said it too loud but I didn't care. "No . . . " I couldn't think in words. "I love you," I cried.

She gathered me in. Deep in her arms I cried and my tears fell against her chest. She rocked me and murmured hushing sounds into my hair until my sobbing ended. I felt the sharp edges of her bones through the frilly housecoat she wore. She was so very thin. How could I not have seen?

She wiped my face with a handful of tissue from the box beside her bed. After awhile, Mr. Morgan and Randy appeared with cocoa and a huge bowl of popcorn. We set up the Monopoly board on the bed and played the game as though everything were fine.

Later, Randy drove me home in the old red pickup. Even though it was almost eleven, our house was dark. Mom was still out cruising with that airhead, Carl. I felt a rush of resentment. My life was crumbling into little pieces all around me. I needed her. But I had closed that door once too often.

Randy shut the truck off and reached for my hand. Any other time, I would have melted into a puddle of embarrassment and nervousness. Now I guess I was just numb all over and glad for his touch.

"You did fine," he said. "A lot of people can't handle

it . . . most of our friends down home stopped coming around when they found out."

"But I didn't handle it well," I whispered. "I almost didn't come back at all."

"But you did," he said quietly.

"Sure, and blubbered like an idiot."

Even in the dark, I could see his sweet smile. "It's O.K. to cry, Persimmona. I cried a lot when I first knew. I still do. Mama understands."

I struggled to ask what I had to know and didn't want to know.

"How . . . how . . . long?"

Randy looked down at my hand that he still held in his. He shrugged. His big shoulders seemed so helpless.

"The doctors say . . . they think probably . . . before Christmas."

I felt my heart squeezed into a tiny ball. Just a week before, I remembered Loretta talking about the smell of Christmas cookies.

"Come see us, Persimmona," Randy said quietly. "Don't be afraid to cry. It helps her to help you . . . can you understand that?"

I nodded. Loretta wanted nothing more out of life than to "do" for others.

Ever so gently Randy's arms slipped around me. It seemed natural to be cradled against his shoulder. I could feel his heart beating. I felt warm and protected.

"You help *me* too," he whispered. "You mean a lot to me, Persimmona."

We sat together for a long time, neither of us wanting to return to the world outside. After awhile, he sighed and reached out to open the truck door. He walked me to the house, saying goodbye with a trembling smile.

As I watched the old red pickup back out of the driveway, I thought about the first day I'd seen him walking toward the bus.

Why did things have to get so mixed up?

The next day, two weeks before Thanksgiving, Randy's dad brought home a ceiling-high fir tree. It filled one whole corner of the bedroom and the sweet smell filled the house. We all pretended that *everyone* put up a Christmas tree six weeks before Christmas.

Loretta clapped her hands in delight as she directed just where to put each light and ornament. She cried when Randy put the angel on the top.

Later, I made a little Santa Claus from a bright red apple, with marshmallows for arms and legs and a head. Cloves dotted the front for the buttons, and made the hands and feet and face. It was something Mom had shown me how to make when I was a little kid—a hundred years before.

Loretta set it on the table next to her bed and said she'd keep it forever. She looked at me when she said it and I knew, and she knew that I knew, that forever wasn't such a very long time.

# CHAPTER 14

On the Sunday after Thanksgiving, I baked Christmas cookies. Me. The original kitchen klutz. My great-grandma Persimmona's recipe for sugar cookies was so simple even a kindergartener could have handled it. I only burned the first pan. The ones after that were a little crispy, but passable. With the old metal cookie cutters Mom had also inherited from her grandma, I cut out Christmas trees and Santa faces and bells. The frosting was runny—I ran out of powdered sugar—but some of it did manage to stick. I was terribly proud of the finished product.

It ran through my mind that maybe good old Great-Grandma Persimmona wasn't such a bad gal after all. If only she'd been named Janet or Suzie or—you get the idea.

With the last of the dough, I cut out a thick, extra-big tree. After it was baked and cool, I trimmed it with bright green frosting and tiny candy hearts. Then I scratched *Mom* into the frosting and set it carefully on the kitchen table where she couldn't miss it.

We'd finally settled into some kind of a cold truce, Mom and I. Anyway, since she was busy with semester finals, we hadn't seen much of each other in the last three weeks. So what else is new?

Thanksgiving had been a tense, mixed-up kind of day. Mom had cooked a chicken and even made a feeble joke about its being an anemic turkey. I waited all afternoon for Creepy Carl to show up. When Mom set the table for just two, I finally asked about him.

"Oh, I think we're getting a little tired of each other," she said with a shrug. She glanced at me from the corner of her eyes and then looked quickly away.

I couldn't hold back the exasperated little noise in my throat. *That's it!* I thought. *Heap the guilt on me! Let me know it's my fault.*

Then she said, "I told him I wanted to spend the day with you . . . just you and me."

So I didn't know whether to feel glad, sad, or guilty. After awhile, though, I wished old Carl had shown up anyway. Mom and I couldn't think of much to say. It was a lonely little dinner. Both of us smiled very hard while we ate, because neither of us wanted the other to be sad. We didn't mention Daddy at all.

We had made it through the next several days without a blow-up. While I baked cookies, Mom was in her office finishing up her semester journalism paper. The old typewriter was clattering at a dangerous speed.

After cleaning up the mess in the kitchen, I carefully packed half the cookies into a plastic bowl. I was anxious about going over to the Morgans'. Mr. Morgan's sister and brother-in-law had come from Mississippi for the Thanksgiving holiday. I'd stayed away. It was exhausting for Loretta to have people around. I didn't want to add to the confusion.

I pulled my jacket on and for a moment, debated whether or not to tell Mom I was going. Finally, I decided not to spoil what little ground we'd gained. I knocked timidly and opened the flimsy door.

She looked up at me, her fingers poised over the typewriter keys. There was a pencil clenched firmly in her teeth like a bit on a horse. Her hair was hanging in her eyes and her eyes were glazed. I thought she looked slightly deranged.

"Uh . . . I'm going to the Morgans' for awhile . . . O.K.?"

She nodded. The glazed look never left her eyes. I shut the door, knowing that when she came to, she'd have no idea where I was. Or what day it was, for that matter.

The day was overcast—cold and crunchy. I held the container of cookies close to me, hoping they'd stay warm and fragrant.

At the end of our driveway, I risked a glance toward Kim's house. Earlier in the day, I'd heard Rich Lawson's old hot rod roar past. Now I could see it still sitting in front of the Douglas house.

Kim's dad had moved out the week before Thanksgiving. Great timing. Men seem to be good at that.

Today, Ms. Douglas' car was gone, too. Just Kim and Rich there. Alone. It made me sick to my stomach. I couldn't think about it anymore. I turned and hurried down the road.

I was just to the blacktop when Rich's car pulled up alongside, idling roughly.

"Well, hello, they-ah, Pu-u-rsimmona," a voice drawled in a sick imitation of Randy's southern speech. I looked just long enough to see it was a creep I didn't recognize. Kim was sitting between him and Rich. I kept on walking.

"Come on, Persimmona," Rich said, laughing. "He's

just teasing." He pulled the car closer until it was at my elbow. "Larry thinks you're cute. How about going for a little ride."

I heard the other guy snort all the way across the seat, and I felt my cheeks go red, but I didn't look at them.

"Leave her alone. She doesn't want to go." It was Kim's voice. My heart tripped over itself.

"Sure she does. Watch." Rich turned the car until the fender blocked my way. He held a beer can out to me. "Here, kid. You don't know what fun is until you try some of this."

"Come on, Rich!" Kim's voice was louder. "Leave her alone."

I couldn't stand it. I turned and bent to look in the window, ignoring Rich.

"Kim? Why don't you go with me?" I stammered. "We'll go to the Morgans' and eat cookies and popcorn and play Monopoly."

They all stared at me silently. I felt like a stupid idiot.

"We can sing Christmas carols, Kim," I blubbered on, my voice getting louder. "Just as we used to do." *When we were children*, I thought. *When we were children.*

"Kim? We can . . . " My voice trailed off to nothing.

Kim was looking at me and for the shortest part of a second, I thought I saw something in her eyes—maybe a little of the old Kim staring back. Then like a shade being pulled down, she shut me out. The eyes became flat and lifeless again. She leaned across Rich's lap, her face just inches from mine.

"Know what my dad said to Mom as he carried his suitcase out last week?" Her voice made chills run up and down my arms. "He said, 'I'm really glad to be rid of you and that crazy kid.' Marvelous parting line, wasn't it?" She laughed but it wasn't a laugh at all. "Wasted space, Lib. Nothing but wasted space."

She put her arm around Rich's shoulders. "Let's go," she told him.

He rolled the window up in my face. The tires squalled and gravel sprayed around me as the car fishtailed away.

The cookies were cold by the time I got to the Morgans'—cold as the pit of my stomach. But when Randy opened the door, I felt a welcome warmth spreading through my whole body.

"Merry Christmas, ho-ho-ho," I said. I held the cookies out. Then I saw his face start to crumple. My knees went weak. Randy was white, his eyes dark with fatigue and red-rimmed.

"Persimmona . . . " he said helplessly.

I ran past him into the bedroom. It looked almost the same. The Christmas tree stood in the corner, its lights blinking bravely, the presents underneath all brightly wrapped and decorated with bows. The television in the other corner featured a rerun of an old Bing Crosby movie, the sound turned down to nothing, the actors pantomiming across the screen.

On one side of the bed, Randy's dad sat in a chair, looking like a sack of flour that had been set down too hard. His head lolled to one side, his sleeping face lined with exhaustion.

On the other side of the bed stood a monster—a metal box attached to an ugly green cylinder. A plastic tube led from the box to Loretta's head. It wrapped around both sides of her face and ended in tiny prongs inserted into her nose. In the quiet room, I could hear a gentle hissing—such a small, unassuming sound. Why did it seem to fill the room?

Eyes closed, Loretta lay motionless in the huge bed, her thin frame made even smaller by the blankets and pillows. She was so still. So still.

If it hadn't been for Randy's hands on my arms, I would have buckled into a heap on the floor.

"It's oxygen," he whispered into my ear. "She started having trouble breathing yesterday, just after Aunt Lenore left. I think she might have been really sick all weekend but she didn't want my aunt and uncle to know."

Oh yes, I thought. It was just like Loretta. Heaven forbid that anyone would be inconvenienced or upset by the fact that she was dying. I swallowed hard.

The long golden eyelashes fluttered.

"Randy?" The soft voice was barely a whisper. He was by her side in an instant.

"I'm here, Mama," he said. He looked at me, his eyes asking a silent question. I took a deep breath and nodded.

"Persimmona's here, too. She baked cookies for us."

I was still holding the stupid cookies. I set them down on the table next to the bed.

A ghost of a smile came to Loretta's lips. "Persimmona, Sugar," she whispered. "Come here." She raised her hand the tiniest bit and I took it. It was small and white and unbelievably frail, and I held it as gently as I could. Her eyes opened and they were brilliant and blue and I could see her in them—far, far away. She spoke carefully and with great effort. I leaned close to hear.

"If I'd had a daughter," she said, "she would have been you."

My vision blurred suddenly and something splashed on the back of my hand.

"Don't grieve for me, Love. I'll be in such a fine place, don't you know? Where I'll be strong and well."

Her eyes closed and she pulled the oxygen into her lungs with short gasps. When she spoke again, it took all her strength.

"Now go home, Sugar. Please. Do you understand? Go home and stay there."

The quiet hissing filled the room with sounds. I looked at Randy. He nodded. I leaned down to kiss her forehead, feeling my heart twist as she smiled. Then I gently laid her hand next to her side.

Randy walked me to the door. He held my hand. We couldn't look at each other.

"It helps to remember that she's in no pain now," he whispered. "It's us . . . the ones she's leaving behind . . . who have to live with the hurt."

When I reached the blacktop, I shoved my fist against my mouth to hold back the stupid gulping noise that kept bubbling from my chest.

I lay down in the grass up by the cornfield fence and stared up at the gray-cloud sky.

Wasted space. That's what I was, all right. She didn't want me there. I couldn't help her live. I couldn't help her die.

# CHAPTER 15

I guess I made it through the week O.K. To be honest, I don't remember much about it. Except that Randy wasn't on the bus or in school.

I wanted to be with the Morgans. I didn't want to be with the Morgans. I kept telling myself I was just obeying Loretta's wishes by staying away. Inside, I knew I wasn't strong enough to be there. She was facing her death with all her remaining strength and courage. There was none left over to comfort me.

By Sunday, I couldn't stand it anymore. The day was gray and cold and windy. Five times I put my coat on. Once I even had my hand on the doorknob. Five times I put the coat back in the closet.

*Go home and stay there, Sugar. Do you understand?*

*Yes, I understand. No . . . no . . .*

Late in the afternoon, I lay down on my bed. Mom came upstairs two or three times to look in the door. Once, she put her hand on my forehead. But she didn't ask me what was wrong.

The room turned dark with night and an approaching storm. In the southwest, thunder boomed. The perfume bottles on my dresser shivered and jingled a nonsense tune on their glass tray. Lightning flashed quick black-and-white images on the wall opposite the window, as though someone outside were flicking a spotlight on and off. The bare limbs of the old oak next to the house played shadow games throughout my room, as the late-fall storm rumbled and complained its way toward me.

I rolled over and pulled the blanket around my ears. The first icy drops chattered against my window.

Without closing my eyes, I saw Loretta's face, her smile big and warm.

*Don't grieve for me, Love*, she whispered. *I'll be in such a fine place, don't you know? Where I can be strong and well.*

The face became Mom's and was filled with a different kind of pain.

*Would you be this upset if it were me instead of her, Persimmona?*

The blanket was too warm and I threw it off, but I couldn't turn off the projector in my head. The film continued to roll.

Dad stood before me, tall and handsome—tanned from the Florida sun.

*Well . . . hello, there!* he said. *How are you . . . ah . . . what was your name again?*

My eyes flew open, but now the face was Kim's and still I couldn't shut it off. Just a reflection on a black bottomless pool, wavering and changing, the image disappearing now and again into the ripples as though she were slowly sinking.

*She needs a friend.* Loretta said it. *She needs you.*

But it was Kim who had built the wall, wasn't it? Hadn't she been the one to shut *me* out?

The ache inside my chest twisted and curled like a cold snake. Why did it have to hurt so bad to grow up?

116

The howling wind almost drowned the sound of the truck pulling into the driveway. The headlights flashed across my window and pulled up close to the back door. The engine continued to run as the door opened and slammed shut.

I swung my legs over the edge of the bed and walked downstairs in the dark like a zombie. I waited in front of the door until he knocked.

The wind whipped in every direction around his face, lashing his long blond hair across his cheeks and eyes. The sleetlike raindrops mixed with the tears streaking his face.

He stared at me.

I felt Mom's hands on my arms, holding me so tightly it hurt. I wanted to cuddle into her lap with my fuzzy blanket pressed against my cheek the way I'd done when I was three after I fell on the cement in the driveway and skinned my knee.

But I was fourteen and taller than my mom, and the fuzzy blanket was just a memory. A hug and a bandage weren't going to make it all right this time.

"She died an hour ago," Randy said. "Would you go for a ride with me?"

I nodded and went to get my coat.

It surprised me that Mom didn't object when I walked out the door. She didn't even ask where we were going. She probably knew I had no idea and that Randy didn't either. When we reached the end of the driveway I looked back. She was standing in the doorway, her body outlined by the yellow kitchen light behind her. I felt an ache in my throat.

The old truck roared down to the blacktop, the wind beating on the windshield with a vengeance. The

117

wipers thunked back and forth wildly, but I still couldn't see a thing. Then I decided it didn't matter. No one else would be out on the road at this hour—in this storm.

At the corner, Randy floored the accelerator and the rear end sloughed sideways in the loose gravel. He looked at me, a tiny smile wobbling on his lips. Then we just drove. Through the sleeping town, around the high school, back out into the country—everywhere— nowhere.

Once he reached over and took my hand. I could feel him tremble.

Finally, the storm's cold fury was spent. Icy drops still shivered and fell from the branches of the oaks surrounding my house. The sound of their splattering on the truck roof was the only noise in the quiet dark when Randy brought me home. He turned the key, shut the lights off, and held me close to him. His body was shaking.

"She loved you, Persimmona," he whispered into my hair after awhile. "We all do."

I could hear Loretta add *don't you know?*

"What will you do now?" My voice sounded thin and sharp, like an overtightened guitar string.

"We'll take her home," he said.

Home was Mississippi, where the winters weren't mean and hard. Somewhere for Loretta, I thought suddenly, it would be summer still—summer always.

I felt Randy's heart beating against my own. "I'll never see you again," I told him.

He sat back and held me at arms' length. "Never say never, Persimmona," he said. Then he leaned close and kissed me. I could taste tears on his sweet lips.

It was everything I thought my very first kiss would

be. A few weeks before, I would have sworn eternal love—started scribbling secret wedding plans and a list of names for the babies.

Now I knew he was very dear to me and I would miss him.

I watched through the glass pane on the back door until the red taillights disappeared. Then I took a deep breath and looked around the kitchen. My hands were heavy. I didn't know where to put them. I wandered in the dark to the living room.

Mom was curled up on her side on the sofa, her hands tucked between her knees. She looked so tiny. Her golden hair curled softly across her cheek and her face was smooth and unlined. It struck me that it was the first time I'd seen the worry lines gone from around her eyes.

*What would I do if she left me? What if it had been her tonight instead of Loretta?*

The thought hit me like a fist in the stomach. I gasped for breath, clasping my arms tightly across my chest. All the dreadful things I'd said and done lately flashed through my mind like the life of a drowning person. What if it had been her and I were standing here now with no way to say I was sorry—no way to take back the things I regretted with all my heart?

A heaviness in my body made my knees tremble. Is this how Randy felt? I remembered Loretta's wistful remark, "We used to fuss and fight with the best of them . . . " But they were so kind to one another, so loving after the doctor's sorrowful diagnosis.

The hurt inside me welled up until I didn't think I could stand it another second. I bent over to keep from groaning out loud. I didn't know what to do or how to feel as I stumbled through the darkened house like a blind person.

Finally I found myself standing in front of the back hall closet.

*You have to be the one who takes the first step,* Loretta told me.

Almost as though they belonged to another person, my hands fumbled through the clothes hanging there until they came to Mom's favorite old sweater. It was ancient, but comfortable and long, hanging almost to her knees when she stood up. She liked to sit in a chair on a cold winter night, her feet curled under her, and tuck the sweater all around. Last year, she'd burned a hole in the front with a cigarette.

It slipped easily off the hanger. I carried it into the kitchen and turned on the light over the stove. In the junk drawer, I found a needle, thread, and scraps of cloth. I chose a piece of red material I remembered had been saved from one of Mom's favorite blouses. A heart was difficult to shape, but I knew that's what I wanted to use.

I threaded the needle and started to sew. Carefully, carefully, neat little stitches the way Loretta had shown me. Not as good as her work, but the very best that I could do.

Sometime—I don't know when—Mom came and sat on the edge of the table next to me. She stroked my hair as I worked. When I was done, I held it up for her to see.

"It's beautiful, Persimmona," she whispered.

She put her arms around me and we cried.

# CHAPTER      16

If you'd asked me, I would have told you that I didn't sleep at all that night. But when the alarm went off, it seemed as if I were floating up to the surface of a brilliantly lit pool. I finally decided it was the sun streaming in through my bedroom window. While I was trying to get my swollen eyes pried open, Mom came in and turned the alarm off. She sat down on the edge of the bed.

I was surprised to see her eyes red and swollen, too. But the smile she gave me was right from the heart.

"I'm not going to work today," she said. "I think I'll just lie around here for a change and relax." She smoothed my hair back out of my face. Her hand was soft and warm.

"You don't have to go to school if you don't want to," she said. "You didn't get much sleep last night."

I yawned and stretched experimentally. The ache was there as I expected—a sharp-edged knot tucked in somewhere between my heart and my stomach—but it wasn't so bad as I'd thought it would be. And as Mom looked at me in that special way, I felt the edges soften and begin to unravel.

"I think I'll be O.K.," I said. I knew she thought I was talking about school. Then she leaned over and kissed me and I wasn't so sure. She went downstairs. In a few minutes I heard cooking noises.

I brushed my teeth and washed my face. My hair would have to do, I thought. I didn't have the energy to climb into the shower. I pulled on a soft wool sweater and a pair of jeans.

For a long time I stood in front of the window. Everything looked so bright, so normal. How could it be? Loretta was gone. How could everything go on—just a few hours later—as though she'd never been?

It hurt. I knew it would hurt forever. I wanted the world to mourn with me. Yet as I looked out at the empty, sun-washed cornfields, I knew it would have been worse to have never known her.

Everything was as it should be—as Loretta would want it to be.

Downstairs in the kitchen, Mom set plates of poached eggs and thin brown toast on the table. I was surprised again to find that I was starved.

When we finished, I helped clear the table and stack the dishes in the sink, without even being asked. I felt a little shy and embarrassed, especially when Mom glanced at me and smiled, but it wasn't so hard to smile back.

Funny thing—it felt good to do something for her—as good as it had felt to do something for Loretta.

The bus would be along in a minute. I began gathering my books together. When I looked out the window, Kim was walking by. She was wearing her old denim skirt. Her hair hung loose, swinging like a pendulum across her back as she clutched her books to her chest and slumped forward. She looked like any of a hundred teenaged girls walking to meet the school bus on a Monday morning.

But she wasn't just anyone. She was my friend.

As clearly as though she stood beside me, I heard Loretta. *Love is meant to be given,* she said. *When you give love, it comes back to you.*

How does a person "do what she has to do"?

*Take the first step.*

But how? What could I do? I'd talked to her—begged . . . . Then, as I watched her walk down the gravel road, I knew.

"Mom!" I yelled. "If the bus comes, wave at Ms. James to wait."

I flew up the steps to my room, jerked my sweater over my head, and slid the jeans down around my ankles. My bedspread was blue with little green flowers.

"Just right for my eyes," I muttered to myself. The knot in my stomach loosened a little bit more.

I wrapped the bedspread around and around until it covered every part of my body but my head, and tied it at my waist with a tassled cord. My gold metal belt made a perfect headband. The extra length hung down to my neck and took the place of dangly earrings.

Mom's makeup was still spread all over the bathroom. I penciled big upsweeps to my eyebrows and smeared some brick-red lipstick over my mouth. The mirror showed me I had exactly the effect I wanted. It was perfect. I had to blink rapidly when I thought how Loretta would love it.

Mom opened her mouth in mute protest as I stumbled back downstairs.

"Please . . . " I said. "Trust me. It's something I have to do."

She started to laugh. Just a chuckle at first. Then deep, side-splitting belly laughs that made tears roll down her cheeks. It was catching. I laughed with her, until both of us were hanging on to each other, shaking.

A feeling I could barely remember welled up inside me—the warm, sweet, hot-fudge-sundae feeling—so unbearably good I couldn't stand too much of it.

"Hey," Mom giggled into my hair. Her voice had a funny catch. "Let's make a bargain. Let's do this at least once a day, no matter what."

"You bet!" I told her.

Mom stepped back, wiping at her eyes. "You look great, P J. I wish your dad could see you."

It took my breath away. Something I'd pushed to a tiny corner of my mind.

*The first step . . .*

I glanced out the window. The bus was coming down the road. I dashed up the stairs again, two at a time, and into my room. I dumped my wastebasket onto my bed and dug out Dad's letter, blessing the part of me that was a slob and kept me from emptying the trash more than twice a year. After I smoothed the paper out as best I could, I pinned it to my bulletin board. Maybe—later on this week, I thought, if I didn't have anything much to do—maybe I'd write. Just a line or two.

Maybe.

I flew down the driveway as the bus pulled up to our stop. The corner of the bedspread streamed out behind me and the loose end of the belt was bruising my ear. I stopped at the bottom of the bus steps, hoping I was doing the right thing.

Ms. James' eyes were wide. "Persimmóna?" she questioned.

For a second, I was stunned! So she knew my name after all!

Then I heard Brian.

"Quick. Someone call Ripley's 'Believe It or Not,'" he said. "Here comes a walking garbage dump."

He continued to run off at the mouth until he noticed I was walking right back to his seat. His voice got lower and lower and trailed away to nothing as I stopped by his elbow.

I didn't stop to wonder what in the world I was doing. I knew if I hesitated, I'd never have the nerve again.

"Brian," I said, just loud enough so that everyone could hear. "Did your mother have any children that lived?"

For once in his whole creepy existence, Brian was at a loss for words. The bright pink patches on his cheeks were very gratifying to me.

The back of the bus was pretty quiet, except for a muffled giggle or two. This time it was Brian they were laughing at.

I flounced around, walked back to my old seat in the middle-school section of the bus, and plopped down.

After a minute, I felt someone slide into the seat next to me.

"Hi," Kim said.

"Hi," I said.

"I heard about Randy's mom."

I could only nod in reply. We sat together in silence, staring out the window at the bare fields. I tried to rearrange the bedspread, which seemed to have tightened around my legs.

126

"Nice outfit," Kim said. The corner of her mouth twitched. Then she blurted out, "I don't care if I ever sit back there."

I could tell she meant it.

"Me either," I said. I meant it too.

We looked at each other for a long time. Kim's mouth bent into a crooked semblance of an old smile.

"Persimmona, Sugar," she said softly, in a perfect imitation of Loretta's sweet voice, "you're really somethin'."

"Don't I know," I said, grinning. "I take up a lot of darn good space."

I was thrilled to see Kim laughing again. Somewhere, I knew, Loretta was watching and applauding. I could feel it.

It was true—life wasn't always fair. But I was beginning to see that the Statue of Liberty syndrome wasn't the worst thing in the world to be afflicted with. The real "Libby" seemed to have the right idea—keep hoping and hold the torch high and take a stand. Sooner or later, there would be better days in the harbor.